gage Cornerstones

CANADIAN LANGUAGE ARTS

PMC #4
428
GAG
274955

Anthology 3b

gage EDUCATIONAL PUBLISHING COMPANY
A DIVISION OF CANADA PUBLISHING CORPORATION
Vancouver · Calgary · Toronto · London · Halifax

Canadian Cataloguing in Publication Data

Main entry under title:

Gage cornerstones: Canadian language arts. Anthology, 3b

Writing team: Christine McClymont, et al.
ISBN 0-7715-1199-X

1. Readers (Elementary).   I. McClymont, Christine.
II. Title: Cornerstones: Canadian language arts.
III. Title: Anthology, 3b

PE1121.G27 1998   428.6   C98-932139-8

Permissions Editor: Elizabeth Long

Researchers: Monika Croydon, Catherine Rondina

Bias Consultant: Margaret Hoogeveen

Cover Illustration: Daphne McCormack

Acknowledgments

Every reasonable effort has been made to trace ownership of copyrighted material. Information that would enable the publisher to correct any reference or credit in future editions would be appreciated.

We acknowledge the financial support of the Government of Canada through the Book Publishing Industry Development Program for our publishing activities.

7 "Friends" from *Snippets* by Charlotte Zolotow. © 1973, 1993 Charlotte Zolotow. Reprinted by permission of S©ott Treimel, New York. / **8-15** "The Lighthouse Dog" by Betty Waterton. Illustrated by Dean Griffiths (Victoria: Orca Book Publishers, 1997). Text © 1997 Betty Waterton. Illustrations © 1997 Dean Griffiths. / **18-20** "Life in the North" excerpted from *YES* Magazine (Autumn, 1997). / **22-29** "Marisol and the Yellow Messenger" by Emilie Smith. Illustrated by Sami Suomalainen. Text © 1994 Emilie Smith. Illustrations © 1994 Sami Suomalainen. Published by Annick Press Ltd. / **32-35** "Prairie Seasons" from *A Prairie Year* © 1994 Jo Bannatyne-Cugnet: text, Yvette Moore: art published by Tundra Books. / **38-45** "Runaway Row" by Lindsay Grater. © 1992 Lindsay Grater. Published by Annick Press Ltd. / **48** "The Secret" by Robert Heidbreder. © 1990 Robert Heidbreder. Published by permission of the author. / **52-59** Excerpts from *What Makes a Magnet?* by Franklyn Branley. Illustrated by True Kelley. Text © 1996 Franklyn Branley. Illustrations © 1996 True Kelley. By permission of HarperCollins Publishers. / **62-67** "Science Fun" excerpted from *More Science Surprises from Dr. Zed* by Gordon Penrose. © 1992 Greey de Pencier Books. / **68-75** "Many Kinds of Energy" excerpted from *Light Magic* by Trudy Rising and Peter Williams. © 1994 Trudy Rising, Peter Williams. Published by Greey de Pencier Books. / **78-83** "Bicycle Power" from *Bicycle Book* by Gail Gibbons. © 1995 Gail Gibbons. All rights reserved. By permission of Holiday House, Inc. / **95** "So Will I" by Charlotte Zolotow from *By Myself* selected by Lee Bennett Hopkins. © 1970 Charlotte Zolotow. Reprinted by permission of S©ott Treimel, New York. / **96-104** "More Than Anything Else" by Marie Bradby. Illustrated by Chris K. Soentpiet. Text © 1995 Marie Bradby. Illustrations © 1995 Chris K. Soentpiet. Published by Orchard Books. / **106-109** "A Pioneer Child's Day" excerpted from *A Child's Day* by Bobbie Kalman and Tammy Everts. © 1994 Crabtree Publishing Company. / **112-113** "Begin Again" material from *Doctor Knickerbocker* by David Booth, illustrated by Maryann Kovalski, used by permission of Kids Can Press Ltd., Toronto. Illustrations © 1993 by Maryann Kovalski. / **114-121** "Emma and the Silk Train" by Julie Lawson, illustrated by Paul Mombourquette, used by permission of Kids Can Press Ltd., Toronto. Illustrations © 1997 by Paul Mombourquette. / **126-127** "Make a Balancing Acrobat" from *Pioneer Crafts* by Barbara Greenwood, illustrated by Heather Collins, used by permission of Kids Can Press Ltd., Toronto. Text © 1997 by Barbara Greenwood. Illustrations © 1997 by Heather Collins. / **130-135** "Noon on the Mountain" from *Morning on the Lake* by Jan Bourdeau Waboose, illustrated by Karen Reczuch, used by permission of Kids Can Press Ltd., Toronto. Text © 1997 by Jan Bourdeau Waboose. Illustrations © 1997 by Karen Reczuch. / **148-149** "Rice Squares" recipe from *Let's Celebrate* by Caroline Parry used by permission of Kids Can Press Ltd., Toronto. Text © 1987 Caroline Parry. / **150-152** "The Great Canadian Nutrition Challenge" from Health and Welfare Canada. / **154-155** "That Takes the Cake" from *Mad as a Wet Hen* by Marvin Terban. By permission of Houghton Mifflin. / **156-157** "Human Pretzels" adapted from "Science Rocks the Circus" by Diane Bailey and Drew McKibbon in *OWL* Magazine (May 1997): Vol. 22, No. 4. ©1997 Bayard Presse Canada Inc. Reprinted with permission.

Photo Credits

18 Halle Flygare/VALAN PHOTOS; **19 top, bottom** Stephen J. Krasemann/VALAN PHOTOS; **20 top** Bob Gurr/VALAN PHOTOS, **middle** Chris Avend/Tony Stone Images, **bottom** James R. Page/VALAN PHOTOS; **36 left** Lori Adamski Peek/Tony Stone Images, **middle** Roy Corral/Tony Stone Images, **right** Lori Adamski Peek/Tony Stone Images; **37** W.L. Habel/First Light; **62-65, 71** Ray Boudreau; **66** Dave Starrett; **70, 72** Bill Ivy/Ivy Images; **77** Dave Starrett; **84 top** Joe Banel, **bottom** Frank Siteman/Tony Stone Images; **86-91** From "Reptiles" episode, Kids@Discovery. Used by permission of Exploration Productions, Inc., Discovery Channel, © 1998; **104** Tuskegee University Archives; **106, 107 bottom, 108 top, 109 top** Marc Crabtree; **108 bottom** Ken Faris; **109 bottom** Bobbie Kalman; **122** J.A. Wilinson/VALAN PHOTOS; **123 left, right** JFF/Ivy Images; **136 left** © Jan Bourdeau Waboose, **right** © Craig Hyde Parker; **140** Tim Pelling/Ivy Images; **141 bottom left** Roman Jaskolski/VALAN PHOTOS, **top left** Henry Kalen/Ivy Images, **right** John Edwards/Tony Stone Images; **142 left** Denis Roy/VALAN PHOTOS, **right** Carl Bigras/VALAN PHOTOS; **143 left** BCO/Ivy Images, **top right** Tony Mihok/Ivy Images, **bottom right** Ivy Images; **144 left** Kennon Cooke/VALAN PHOTOS, **right** Ken Fisher/Tony Stone Images, **bottom right** © Ottmar Bierwagen Photo Inc./Canada in Stock Inc./Ivy Images; **145 top left** Kennon Cooke/VALAN PHOTOS, **top right** Linda Rouhinen/Canada in Stock, **bottom right** Lelande Bobbe/Tony Stone Images; **148-149** Dave Starrett; **151-152** Photodisc, Inc; **156-158** Cirque du Soleil/Al Seib/Costumes: Dominque Lemieux.

Illustrations

6-7 Patrick Fitzgerald; **17** Dean Griffiths; **18** John Etheridge; **31** Joe Weissman; **47, 92-93** Steve Attoe; **48-49** Dušan Petričić; **50-51** Gord Mercer; **61** True Kelley; **65, 67** Tina Holdcroft; **66, 110-111, 159** Bill Suddick; **68-69, 73-75** Jane Kurisu; **94-95** Laurie McGaw; **105** Margaret Hathaway; **124 top** Kids Can Press, **bottom left** cover design by Christine Toller, cover art by David Powell, **bottom right** cover design by Christine Toller, cover art by Judy McLaren; **125** Paul Mombourquette; **128** Heather Collins; **129** Dayle Dodwell; **138-139** Kim La Fave; **146-147** David Bathurst; **150** Anne Stanley. Adapted from Canada's Food Guide to Healthy Eating, Health Canada, 1992. With permission of the Minister of Public Work and Government Services Canada, 1998. **154-155** Clarence Porter.

ISBN 0-7715-1199-X
 3 4 5 6 BP 03 02 01 00
Printed and bound in Canada.

Cornerstones Development Team

WRITING TEAM

Christine McClymont
Patrick Lashmar
Dennis Strauss
Josephine Lashmar
Patricia FitzGerald-Chesterman
Cam Colville
Robert Cutting
Stephen Hurley
Luigi Iannacci
Oksana Kuryliw
Caroline Lutyk

GAGE EDITORIAL

Joe Banel
Rivka Cranley
Elizabeth Long
Evelyn Maksimovich
Diane Robitaille
Darleen Rotozinski
Jennifer Stokes
Carol Waldock

GAGE PRODUCTION

Anna Kress
Bev Crann

DESIGN, ART DIRECTION & ELECTRONIC ASSEMBLY

Pronk&Associates

ADVISORY TEAM

Connie Fehr Burnaby SD, BC
Elizabeth Sparks Delta SD, BC
John Harrison Burnaby SD, BC
Joan Alexander St. Albert PSSD, AB
Carol Germyn Calgary B of E, AB
Cathy Sitko Edmonton Catholic SD, AB
Laura Haight Saskatoon SD, SK
Linda Nosbush Prince Albert SD, SK
Linda Tysowski Saskatoon PSD, SK
Maureen Rodniski Winnipeg SD, MB
Cathy Saytar Dufferin-Peel CDSB, ON
Jan Adams Thames Valley DSB, ON
Linda Ross Thames Valley DSB, ON
John Cassano York Region DSB, ON
Carollynn Desjardins
    Nipissing-Parry Sound CDSB, ON
David Hodgkinson Waterloo Region DSB, ON
Michelle Longlade Halton CDSB, ON
Sharon Morris Toronto CDSB, ON
Heather Sheehan Toronto CDSB, ON
Ruth Scott Brock University, ON
Elizabeth Thorn Nipissing University, ON
Jane Abernethy Chipman & Fredericton SD, NB
Carol Chandler Halifax Regional SB, NS
Martin MacDonald Strait Regional SB, NS
Ray Doiron University of PEI, PE
Robert Dawe Avalon East SD, NF
Margaret Ryall Avalon East SD, NF

Contents

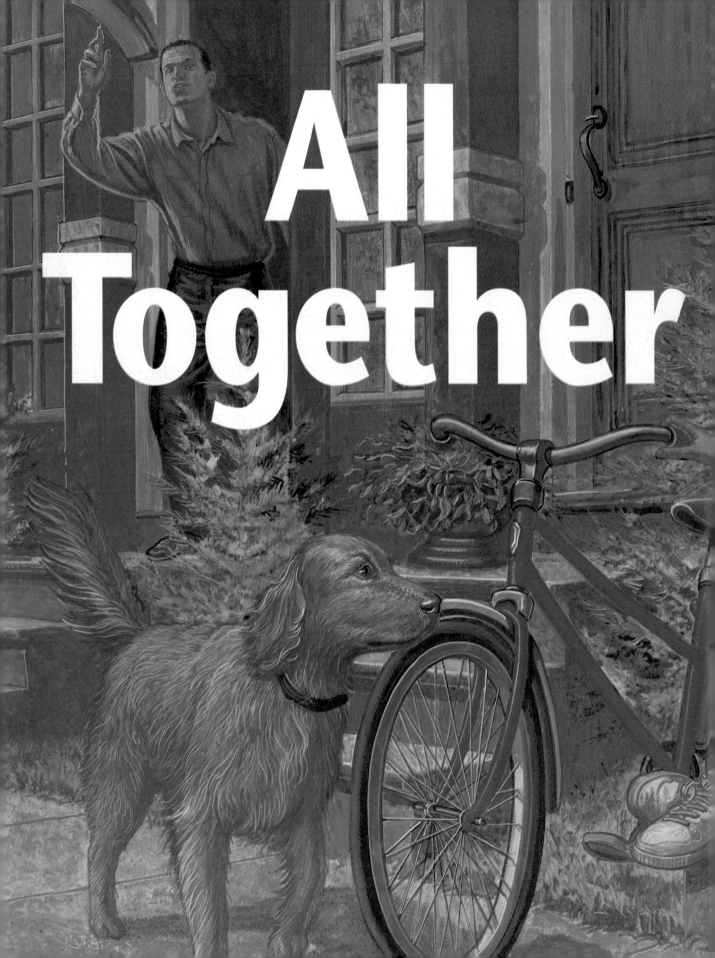

Friends

Poem by **Charlotte Zolotow**

We can sit on the steps
in the sun
and not say anything.
It's nice.
But when I go home,
I sometimes can't wait for dinner to end
so I can call you.
But sometimes you call me first.

What kind of dog would you like? What kind of dog do you think people who live in a lighthouse would like?

The Lighthouse Dog

Story by
Betty Waterton

Pictures by
Dean Griffiths

One day the captain's wife, Hildegarde, put her town hat on her head, her town shoes on her feet, and her shopping bag over her arm. "Today is market day in town, and I'm going to get a puppy," she told her husband. "My friend Flossie is going to help me choose it, and oh, I can hardly wait!"

"Well, if you must, you must," sighed the captain. "But just get a small one."

"I will," said Hildegarde.

As she climbed into her little rowboat, he said, "And don't forget to bring home a pizza for supper. A large one!"

"I won't," she promised. And with the oars in the oarlocks gently squeaking, she rowed away from the lighthouse.

As she neared the town, Hildegarde saw someone with frizzy hair jumping up and down on the dock. It was her friend Flossie.

"Hurry, hurry!" shouted Flossie. "Or they'll all be gone!"

But when they got to the market, they found there were still lots of puppies left. Black ones, brown ones, yellow and white—some with spots and some with splotches. And one really BIG dark one.

"I can't choose," cried Hildegarde. "I love them all! But I especially love that really big practically black one with the pink necktie."

"That's not a necktie, that's her tongue," said Flossie. "She's almost a real Newfie. I think."

"I do love her the most, but she's SO BIG..."

"She just seems big," said Flossie. "You could name her 'Molly,' after my grandmother on my mother's side."

"I love that name," said Hildegarde.

So Hildegarde bought the big dog and named her Molly. She bought a big bag of dog crumbles and some jumbo milk bones. Then she and Flossie had a nice fish-and-chips lunch.

"Don't forget the pizza," said Flossie. "Get one with olives."

So Hildegarde bought a Super-Duper-Special-De-Luxe salami pizza with olives to take home to the captain. Then they all went back to the boat.

"Thanks for all your help, Flossie," shouted Hildegarde, as she rowed away. But her friend Flossie had already gone— back home to help her mother make beeswax candles.

Meanwhile, the captain had finished doing all his lighthouse things. He had made himself a bowl of almost-instant seaweed soup for lunch, and now he was dozing on the beach, dreaming of pizzas.

He woke up when he heard the splashing of oars in the water. There was Hildegarde, rowing wearily toward him, her hat all askew. And there was someone in a practically black fur coat. A fur coat?!!

Suddenly there was a gigantic splash as Molly jumped out of the boat and into the water. She swam to shore, shook herself, and lumbered over to the captain. Putting her front paws on his shoulders, she mopped his face lovingly with her big, pink tongue. The captain toppled over backwards.

"This is Molly, our new puppy," said Hildegarde, as she helped him up. "Flossie says she's almost a real Newfoundland."

"That's a puppy?" cried the captain, wiping his face with his handkerchief.

"Sort of an old puppy, I guess. Flossie says she just seems big. Now, come into the house and see what I bought you."

Smacking his lips, the captain peered into the shopping bag. But all that was left of the Super-Duper-Special-De-Luxe salami pizza were some crumbs and five olives.

"Oh, dear," said Hildegarde. "Well, at least now we know Molly doesn't like olives. But not to worry, I'll make you some almost-instant seaweed soup."

"I'm getting mighty tired of that," grumbled the captain.

Molly ate two dishpans full of dog crumbles. Then she took Corky the cat off the chesterfield and placed him on top of the piano. After that, she stretched out on the chesterfield herself, and went to sleep.

The next day Molly carried Corky the cat outside and put him, yowling, into the little rowboat. She towed it around to the far side of the island and hid the oars in the bushes. She dumped Corky's cat crumbles into the sea. She ate Hildegarde's hat, and buried her town shoes under some kelp.

"She's just feeling insecure," said Hildegarde. "She's afraid she's going to be sent back to town."

When they found sixteen starfish and a baby crab in their bed, the captain merely grunted. And when he found his favourite furry slippers all sticky around the edges, he groaned. But when Molly ate their whole Thanksgiving dinner—including the pumpkin pie—he cried, "That's it. Enough!"

Hildegarde sighed and blew her nose. "I guess Molly isn't working out too well, is she?"

"You might say that," said her husband. "I think you'd better take her back to the market tomorrow."

But the next morning when they looked outside, there were whitecaps on the water. "It's too rough today," said the captain.

The day after that the sea was an ominous dark green, and purple clouds scudded across the sky. "There's a storm coming," he told his wife. "You certainly can't go to town today."

On the third day the wind blew salt spray against the windows. The lighthouse beacon flashed and the big bell on the rocks clanged. "I hope there is nobody out there in this storm," said the captain.

But that very evening Hildegarde suddenly cried out, "I think I hear somebody calling…"

The captain opened the door and listened. "So do I! There is somebody out there! I must rescue them!"

He took his lantern, and raced down to the dock. The waves were washing right over it.

From somewhere out on the water, a voice called: "HELP!"

"I'M COMING!" The captain jumped into his lifesaving boat and pulled the starter cord. Again and again he pulled it. But the motor would not start.

Just then Molly hurtled past him. She plunged into the crashing sea and began swimming. Then she was gone—into the black, stormy night.

Swinging his lantern, the captain paced back and forth on the beach, while the wind howled and the waves crashed. Then, in the light of a lightning flash, he saw something swimming toward him. It was Molly. There was someone clinging to her, clutching her thick fur.

Back inside the warm lighthouse, the rescued
fisherman huddled by the fire, wrapped in blankets.
As he sipped his hot almost-instant seaweed soup,
he marvelled over his rescue.

"That's what Newfies do,"
said the captain, proudly.

Molly became known as
the Lighthouse Dog, and only
once did she ever go back to
town. That was the day
she received her shiny, almost
silver lifesaving medal from
Hildegarde's friend Flossie's
uncle on her father's side,
the mayor. ●

Were you surprised by the dog Hildegarde chose? What kind of home would not suit a Newfoundland dog?

Understanding the Story

Molly to the Rescue

- What is the worst trouble Molly gets into?
- How does Molly know what to do in the storm?
- Do you think Molly will ever get into trouble again? Explain your answer.

Language Study

WRITING CONVERSATION

Betty Waterton uses lots of conversation to make her story lively. She doesn't always write "he said" or "she said." Notice how "sighed" and "shouted" help you to hear the speakers' voices.

"Well, if you must, you must," sighed the captain.

"Hurry, hurry!" shouted Flossie.

Complete these sentences in your notebook. Use words that help you to hear the speakers' voices.

"That's a kitten?"_____ the captain.

"I don't want to clean up my room,"_____Willy.

"Wait for me!" _____ Ozman.

"I'll catch that fly ball!" _____ Lizzie.

Viewing the Illustrations

Choose your favourite illustration.
Now choose the funniest illustration.
Are they the same? With a partner,
discuss why most people like to
laugh.

Media Link — Molly's TV Series

Imagine that you are a television scriptwriter. You want to create a new TV series starring Molly, but you have to sell the idea to a children's TV producer.

Copy this report form into your notebook.

Molly would make a great TV star because _____.

The lighthouse setting is exciting because _____.

I can think of at least three great stories Molly could star in: _____.

Besides the captain and Hildegarde, I would add these characters: _____.

The best audience would be kids aged _____ to _____ .

Fill in the form with ideas that will persuade
the producer to make your series.

What do you think it would be like to live in northern Canada?

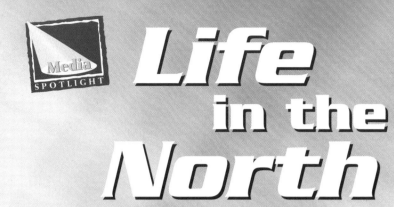

Life in the North

What is it really like to live in the North? *YES Mag* (a science magazine for kids) asked kids who read the magazine to let them know. Here are some of their letters.

Letters by
CANADIAN KIDS

Dear YES Mag,

I like living in Hay River because in the summer I can swim in Great Slave Lake (see photo). In the winter I can cross-country ski at the golf course. I enjoy sledding and skating, as well. What I don't like are the bugs in the summer, and it gets really cold in January.

Hay River is special because it used to be a tropical sea 350 million years ago and because it is rich in fossils. As you walk through town along the river, you can find coral and clamlike fossils.

In the summertime, it is warm, around 25° to 30°C. In the winter, there are cold spells of about -40°C. I can see the northern lights at night.

Alex MacLean, 8
Hay River, Western Territory

Dear YES Mag,

In Dawson City, we try to make things look old-fashioned by having wooden houses and wooden sidewalks.

Some people think we live in ice houses and hunt for food. But we go to school and live in houses and buy food. I have lived in Dawson all my life.

My dislikes are that it's cold, it's too small, there are no malls, and no fast food. My likes are that it's quiet, pretty, safe, everybody knows you, and there is only one school.

In 1897, people from all over the world came here to look for gold and strike it rich. Tourists still come every summer to see Dawson. We also have northern lights here—they are very pretty. They are green, blue, and yellow. The scientific name for them is **aurora borealis**.

Stephanie Matchett, 10
Dawson City, Yukon

Dawson City Post Office

Celebration in Dawson City

Life in the North   **19**

Dear YES Mag,

I live in Fort Smith, which is by the Slave River and is surrounded by forest. I like to go down to the rocks by the rapids and watch the pelicans that nest on the islands in the river. This is the most northern pelican colony in North America.

There are several bison herds around Fort Smith. My dad is the bison ecologist, and in the spring I petted some newborn bison calves.

It's great living in the North, and one of the best things is watching the northern lights on clear nights in the fall and winter.

Matthew Gates, 10
Fort Smith, Western Territory

Bison herd

Inuit children enjoying a blanket toss

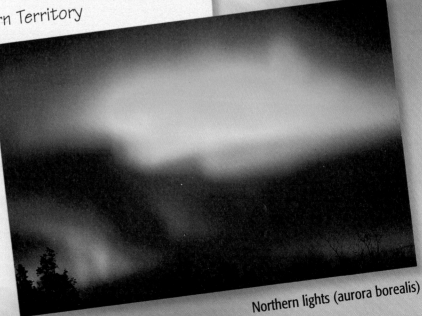

Northern lights (aurora borealis)

FOLLOW UP

If you could visit one of these kids, which one would you choose? Why? What would you like to do with him or her?

Understanding the Selection

Northern Lights

Find proof in the letters for each of these sentences.

- Northern kids are just like you.
- Dawson City is a popular tourist spot.
- In the North it gets very hot in summer and very cold in winter.
- You can find unusual wildlife in the North.

Reading a Map

Look at a map of northern Canada. Answer these questions about the letter writers.

- Which of the towns is the farthest north?
- Which of the rivers is longest?
- How do you think Great Slave Lake got its name?

Choose one of these places and discuss with your family members what you know about it.

A Letter

Write a letter to one of the northern letter writers. Tell him or her about the place where you live. Talk about what makes this place special, what you like to do, and what you don't like to do.

Have you ever
moved to a new
place? How did you
feel? Was it hard to
make new friends?

Marisol
and the
Yellow Messenger

This is the story of a girl called Marisol.
In Spanish, Marisol means ocean and sun.
Her parents gave her this name because
when she was born she was happy and warm
like the morning sun, and her eyes and hair were
black like the deep ocean on a moonless night.

STORY BY
Emilie
Smith

PICTURES BY
Sami
Suomalainen

But a day came when her eyes changed and told their own sad story. When Marisol was only eight years old her father was killed, and she, her mother, and her little brothers had to run away to Canada. Every single day and every night the only thing she thought about was her beautiful country and all the things her father had taught her before he died.

Now they were in a strange country, where people spoke a different language. They lived on the first floor of a two-storey house on a busy street, with a laundromat on one side of them, and a grocery store on the other. Marisol didn't go out much. She played with her brothers, but they were small. Sometimes she tried to help her mother.

One day, Marisol was coming home from school.
It was getting dark even though it was only afternoon,
and her breath made thin clouds in front of her face.
She shivered as the icy snow drifted down, and she
shuffled her cold feet. The snow was dirty from the
cars and trucks that rumbled past.

She sighed and imagined herself back in her
grandparents' house—
she was rocking with her
grandpa in the hammock
after school, listening to
the rhythm of the slap,
slap of her grandma
making tortillas.

She shook off the daydream when she reached her house. The family ate supper and watched some TV, but after awhile, tired of listening to English, they went to bed.

That night there came a great storm. The wind moaned and the snow blew around in big gusts and blinding circles. Marisol was listening to the whistling of the storm.

She began to think again of her grandfather and grandmother; then she looked at the big picture of her father above her bed and cried for awhile. Then she fell asleep.

When the whole house and the street outside were still, Marisol began to dream. She saw four old women kneeling on the ground. They were weaving, pulling the weft thread through the warp, their brown hands working quietly, quickly. The women were dressed in brilliant reds, greens, pinks, blues, and yellows. They were women from her homeland, and the cloth they were weaving had every colour of the world in it. Marisol was in the middle of their circle and they spoke with her.

"You know us, Marisol," they said. "We are your great-grandmothers' mothers. We are in the trees and the stars, the jaguars and the corn. We see everything and are touched by everything. Now look inside— your tears are ours, because your father was our son. And when he died our voices sobbed along with yours, the aching drums sounded from within our bodies. We come to bring you peace.

See how your father is with us now, and with you always. His breath is the wind that lifts your hair. His eyes are the stars that are watching you. So look for him everywhere, and don't be afraid, pequeña*."

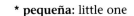

---

* **pequeña:** little one

As she lay in their circle, Marisol felt safe and protected, and for the first time a deep pain in her body began to flow out. She looked from one face to another, and the cloth that the women were weaving grew wide. It grew bigger than themselves and Marisol was surrounded by a giant multicoloured circle.

Then she woke up.

It was dark outside. The storm had calmed, and she listened to the breathing of one brother, then the other, then to the gentle sighs of their mother in the small room they all shared. She couldn't quite remember the dream, but she felt warm in her bed. Soon she fell asleep again.

The next day, the whole big city was covered in snow—so much snow that cars stopped moving and school was cancelled. People got busy digging, and happy children bundled up and went climbing in the mountains of snow. Marisol and her brothers went out. They played in the snow as though they had lived in the North all their lives. They made snowballs and went sledding with the other children.

Finally, as the sun was going down, they ran home tired, cold, and laughing.

On the way down the street, Marisol remembered the dream. She remembered the words of the old women "...so look for him everywhere." She looked around at the stillness of the snow. She did not see her father's face anywhere in the frozen white. The children arrived breathless at the front stairs. The little boys went in, pulling off their boots and talking both at once to their mother. But Marisol didn't go straight in. She stood at the door, waiting.

At that moment she saw something coming that made her eyes open wide and her hair tingle. Out of the white came a little yellow bird. It came straight toward her, and when she opened the door wide it flew in. There was a great uproar in the tiny apartment as the bird fluttered around, stopping here and there, looking at the people with its little head tilted. They put out some water in a teacup without a handle, and some sesame seeds in the lid of a sour-cream container. The bird landed to take little sips and pecks.

As darkness filled the streets outside, the little visitor calmed down.

"We must let it go again," said Marisol's mother. "It's not fair to hold it prisoner." But Marisol and her brothers pleaded with her to let the creature stay.

"It would die for sure out on a night like this," they said. So the little yellow bird with the cheery black eyes stayed. It spent the night in the warm bathroom, on a perch made out of a wooden spoon.

Before Marisol went to sleep, she checked up on the bird one last time. It had begun to trill, it felt so at home in the warm apartment. As she lay down she listened, and it seemed to her as though the bird were singing, in a voice she had heard so many times before, "Don't be afraid, my little one, don't be afraid, my little one."

Marisol pulled her covers tightly around her. She smiled softly in recognition, and she felt a love for her mother and her little brothers that was stronger than ever before.

She knew why the yellow bird had come. ●

Why was it hard for Marisol to leave her country? If you met her, what would you like to tell her?

Understanding the Story

Ocean and Sun

- What does the name Marisol mean in Spanish?

- Why do Marisol, her mother, and brothers come to Canada?

- Why does Canada feel like a strange place to Marisol?

- Who comes to visit Marisol in her dream? How do they help her?

- When does Marisol start enjoying life in her new home?

- What message does the yellow bird bring to Marisol?

Congratulations! You can join the good reader's club.

WRITING IN YOUR JOURNAL

When Marisol dreams about her ancestors, she feels safe and protected. A deep pain in her body begins to flow out. Have you ever felt sad, and then been comforted? Write in your journal about a time when you felt sad or homesick. When and why did you begin to feel better?

MANY WORDS FOR FRIEND

Some of your classmates may speak more than one language. On the chalkboard, write the word for **friend** in as many languages as you can.

Media Link

Take Action!

If Marisol came to your school, how could you make her feel welcome? With your group, make a plan to help new students feel welcome. For example, you could make a "Welcome to Our School" video to help new students.

You could also create a poster with tips for new students.

Invite your principal to class and share your ideas. Find out if there are any newcomers who may need your friendship.

BEFORE READING

Can you name Canada's prairie provinces? What do you know about life on the Prairies? These pictures tell part of the story.

Prairie Seasons

Picture essay by *Yvette Moore*

Winter

At the rink, children dream of playing in the big leagues.

Spring
Everyone marvels at the softness of the baby chicks.

Summer

For the 4-H Beef competition, each calf is groomed to perfection.

Fall

At Agribition*, lucky is the child allowed to ride with a winning team. ◗

---

* **Agribition:** an agricultural (farming) exhibition

What new things
did you learn
about rural life in
the Prairies from
these pictures?
What else would
you like to know?

Personal Response

Have you heard the saying,

"A picture is worth a thousand words"?

What do you think it means? Do you think it's true of Yvette's pictures? What words do you think of when you look at the pictures?

Your Turn to Draw

Draw four pictures—one for each season.
Show what you like to do in spring, summer, winter, and fall.
Write a few words under each picture. Share these drawings
with someone in your family.

Viewing the Pictures

When they're painting, artists decide what to put in the front of the picture—the **foreground**—and what to put in the back of the picture—the **background**. Things in the foreground look close and things in the background look far away.

Look at the picture called "Winter." The player in the foreground has his back to us.

Up close we see his stick, his teammates, his coach. We want this team to win.

In the background, we see the goalie and some kids on the other team. We don't know so much about them.

Now look at the other pictures. What is in the foreground in each picture? What feelings do these things give you? What is in the background?

What can you learn about the Prairies from these pictures?

A Story

YOUR TURN TO WRITE

Choose one of the pictures in *Prairie Seasons*. What is happening in the picture? What do you think happened just before? What will happen next? Can you turn the picture into a story? Give the people names, and write your story.

Did You Know ?

Many kids who live in the country join the 4-H Club. The four H's stand for Head, Heart, Hands, and Health. To join, kids have to be between nine and nineteen years of age. They have fun, and learn useful things—like how to raise calves, sew, and take photos.

In your own neighbourhood, have you ever seen something old knocked down to make way for something new? How did you feel about it?

Runaway Row

Story and Pictures by
Lindsay Grater

Have you ever been to Ratscuttle Row? It is a street down by the docks, in front of the shoe factory, close to the bicycle factory, opposite the washing machine factory, not far from the soap factory, which is a stone's throw from the nuts and bolts factory.

At one time, there were five little houses on Ratscuttle Row. They spent their time gossiping about the families who lived in them and watching the comings and goings at the factories.

The houses started noticing that the factory workers looked grumpy all the time. They heard that the old buildings were uncomfortable and overcrowded and that some big changes were needed.

So, plans were made to knock down the factories and build modern ones. To gain extra space, the houses were going to be knocked down too.

"We were here long before the factories!" gasped Number 1.

"Why can't they just build around us?" cried Number 2.

"Surely the new shoe factory could manage without those extra square metres!" complained Number 3.

"We have been good and comfortable homes for our people," said Number 4.

"And should be shown some respect for our long years of faithful service," added Number 5.

Soon the work began. Heavy construction machines started thundering along the street. They left muddy tire tracks and dust behind them.

On the other side of town, new houses were being built for the Ratscuttle Row families. At first the people had been sad about leaving their old homes. Now, with all this mess and noise, it would be a relief to go somewhere cleaner and quieter.

As Moving Day approached, the insides of the houses were packed up. The rooms felt bare and echoey.

Finally the moving vans came.

"Goodbye," a little boy called out as he was leaving. "I wish you houses could move to a nice new place too!"

As night fell, the houses missed the happy busy sounds that had always filled them. Only sad sounds reached them now—an ambulance wailing and cats fighting.

They missed the smell of cooking and the gurgle of water in their pipes. They were going to be knocked down the following day and they started to shiver with fear.

"It's been a **good** life," sighed Number 5. "I'm sorry that it's over."

"I looked after my people for years," moaned Number 4 sadly, "but no one is going to look after me."

"You know, I put up with a lot of wear and tear from my family," Number 3 blurted out. "But I never complained."

"I can't bear to think that this is the last night of our lives," wailed Number 2.

"We were good homes," shouted Number 1 angrily, "and we still could be!"

Then the houses started getting quite worked up by listing things they would never see again.

"No more Christmases, no more birthday parties. No more log fires or new wallpaper or new babies!"

They started to vibrate as though an engine had been switched on.

"All we have to look forward to is a great, big, heavy wrecking ball!" growled Number 1. "I wish we could get away from it!"

Just to the left of Venus, a shooting star appeared in the sky. It spiralled toward Earth and, as it looped the loop over the Midsummer Madness Soap Factory, the wishing started to work.

With a plop like a plug being pulled, the houses ripped away from the ground. They made a sharp right turn and scraped along the side of the Cloggo Shoes factory.

Garbage cans in their path were sent flying. Road signs were spun around to point the wrong way. In the park, flower beds were flattened and a statue had its head knocked off.

"Where are we going?" Number 5 spluttered out.

"Who cares?" was Number 1's cheeky reply.

Amazingly, only one person heard the commotion. A night watchman in a warehouse had his hearing aid turned up too high. He thought the rumbling was coming from his tummy and he reached for his snack.

The houses were heading toward the river.

"Anyone for a swim?" joked Number 3 nervously, as they crossed the high and narrow bridge.

Sleepy gulls and pigeons were shaken off the railings and clung to the moving roofs.

When they reached the other side, the houses sighed with relief. That gave them the idea of puffing air up their chimneys and they left the town making silly toot-toot, choofy-choofy sounds.

Out in the countryside, they started getting wild. Whooping and shrieking, they swooped around curves, enjoying their new-found freedom.

Soon the town was just a tiny glow behind them. On and on the train of houses sped. Birds and animals along the way jumped on board.

The land became more hilly. Up and over, down and around they rattled. Suddenly a low bridge appeared around a bend in their path.

"Duck!" yelled Number 1.

"Where?" demanded the others, a split second before the chimneys were slapped flat like five dominoes.

No one seemed to care. With a flat roof, it was possible to go even faster.

The house-express ripped a deep track through a field, shaking more creatures out of their hiding places.

"Who on earth are you?" they squawked.

"Don't you know—we are Ratscuttle Row!" answered Number 5.

"No we're not!" roared the others. "We are Runaway Row, Runaway Row, Runaway, Runaway, Runaway Row!"

And they could still be heard chanting their new name long after they had disappeared.

Ten fields later, at the top of a hill, the houses wheezed to a stop.

The sun rose and the houses basked in its glow while they caught their breath.

"Well," said Number 5 at last, "we got our wish. And we saved everyone the trouble of knocking us down too!"

"What a beautiful spot to land in," sighed Number 4. "We could be very happy here."

"But isn't something missing?" asked Number 3 after a few minutes. "Isn't it all a bit too quiet? Wouldn't a few people make it perfect?"

"If we wait patiently, some will find us," said Number 2 gently.

"Yes, you're right," replied Number 1, "and I have a feeling that we won't have to wait very long..."

How did the houses of Ratscuttle Row avoid being knocked down? Is this solution possible in real life?

Understanding the Story

Runaway Homes

- How do you know Ratscuttle Row is a city street?
- What big changes threaten the old houses?
- What do the empty houses miss most?
- What starts the magic that helps the houses escape?
- What do you think will happen at the end of the story?

Make a City and Country Chart

The houses from Ratscuttle Row notice the mess and the noise in the city. But they also find the country too quiet. Which do you think you would prefer— city or country living? Copy this chart into your notebook. Fill in some good things and not-so-good things about both places.

City or Town Living		Country Living	
Good Things	Not-so-good Things	Good Things	Not-so-good Things

A Story

Have you heard the expression, "If these walls could talk…"?

Pretend that you are a house on your street. You can see, hear, and speak! Write a story about the things you see and hear on your street. Trade your story with a partner. Swap ideas on how to make your stories more interesting. Then write a new, improved version of your story.

TECH LINK
Use a computer to help polish your final draft.

The grass needs cutting, don't you think?

Oh, look! Here comes the mail.

Looks like it might rain.

Have you heard? The Joneses have a new cat.

Cool.

Language Study

NOISY VERBS

Lindsay Grater has used many wonderful "noisy" verbs in her story:

rattled moaned wheezed gasped shrieked thundered

Choose three of these verbs and write three noisy sentences.

Something To Think About

Sometimes in cities, old things get in the way of new things. Some people may want to knock down old houses to make room for big, new buildings. But other people may want to save the old buildings. What would you want to do?

The Secret

Poem by *Robert Heidbreder*

Jim told me a secret
    I shouldn't tell anyone,
But I told it to Julie
    Who thought that it was fun.
And Julie crossed her heart—
    She promised not to say—
But broke her word and told it
    The very next day.
She whispered it to Alex
    Who told it back to Jim
Who's mad at me for telling
    The secret on him.
And now I'm mad at Julie
    (She promised not to tell!)
And Julie's mad at Alex,
    So mad that she could yell.
And Alex glared at Jim
    And said that he was twisted.
Then Jim came straight to me
    And said I would be fisted!
I hope all this blows over.
    I think it should, because
I've totally forgotten
    What the secret was!

Personal Response

• Do you like sharing secrets with friends? How does it make you feel?

• Have you ever told a secret when you didn't mean to? What happened?

Tell a Story

Turn the poem into a story. How will the kids in the poem become friends again? Will you reveal Jim's secret? Have fun!

MORE GOOD READING

🍁 **The Patchwork House**
by Sally Fitz-Gibbon
This is the story of a house, and all the families that come to live in it. (a picture book story)

Grandfather's Dream
by Holly Keller
A community has to decide between growing rice and bringing the cranes back to the village.
(a picture book story)

Hopscotch Around the World
by Mary D. Lankford
Learn how children in India, Poland, Nigeria, France, and many other countries play hopscotch.
(a non-fiction picture book)

Flip through the pages of this article. Look for the title and the sub-heads on pages 55 and 56. What will you be learning about in this article? What will you be doing?

Article by
Franklyn Branley

Pictures by
True Kelley

What Makes a Magnet?

Read this article before you do what it says.

Let's go fishing with a magnet.

Put different things in a box: a penny, a nickel, and a dime; a twig, some tacks and paper clips, bits of aluminum foil, rubber bands, pieces of paper, and a pin or two.

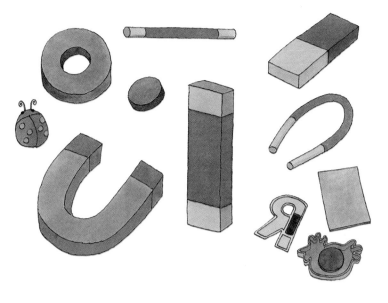

Next, find a magnet. They come in different shapes and sizes.

Tie one end of a string around your magnet. Tie the other end to a stick or a pencil. This is your fishing pole.

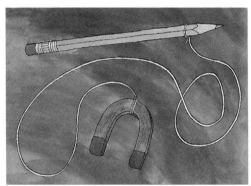

Go fishing in the box. Put the things you "catch" in a pile. The other things will stay in the box.

Everything you lifted out of the box is made of iron: the tacks, the paper clips, and the pin. The magnet won't pick up a twig, rubber bands, aluminum foil, paper, a dime, a nickel, or a penny because they are not made of iron. Dimes, nickels, pennies, and aluminum foil are made of other kinds of metal. A magnet only picks up things that have a lot of iron in them.

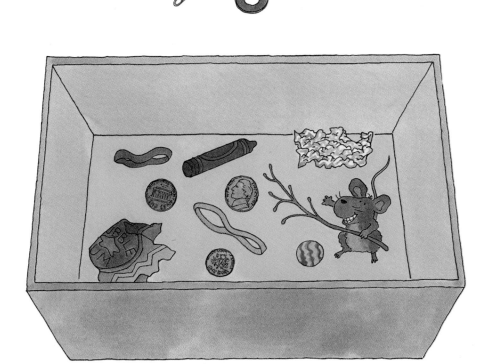

Make Your Own Magnet

You can make your own magnet with a needle. Needles are made of steel, which is mostly iron.

Hold the eye of the needle.

Stroke the needle along one end of the magnet. Move along the magnet in only one direction: from the eye of the needle to the point, not back and forth. Do this twenty or thirty times.

Touch the end of the needle to a tack, a paper clip, or another needle. Your needle will lift them up. You have made a magnet.

The bigger and stronger a magnet is, the more objects it will pick up at once.

Make Your Own Compass

Your needle magnet is a little one. But there are very large magnets. In fact, the whole Earth is a magnet. And you can prove it.

1 First, use your needle magnet to make a compass. Get two small pieces of foam plastic, or cork, and stick a piece on each end of the needle.

CAREFUL— don't stick yourself.

CORK   NEEDLE MAGNET   CORK

2

Then float the needle in a bowl of water. The needle will swing around so one end points north. Keep the needle in the centre of the bowl, so it can swing freely. Turn the needle around. When you let go, the same end will again point north.

3

Put a dot of ink on that end. You have made a compass.

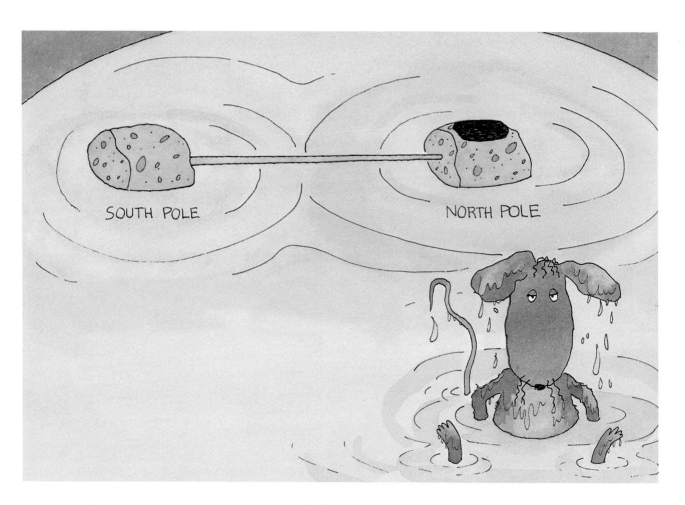

SOUTH POLE

NORTH POLE

The ends of the magnet are different. One is called the north-seeking pole, or simply the north pole. On your compass, it's the one with the ink dot on it. The other end is the south-seeking pole, or simply the south pole.

Magnets are strongest at the poles. When you picked things out of your fishing box, they stuck to the ends of the magnet, not the middle.

HEY!

What Makes a Magnet? **57**

Your compass points north because the Earth is a magnet. The north-seeking pole of your compass points toward the north pole of the Earth magnet. No matter how you turn your compass, it will always point north when you let go of it.

The Earth is a magnet because it contains a lot of iron. The moon does not have as much iron, so it is not a magnet. Your compass would not work on the moon.

When people go hiking in the woods, they take a compass with them so they don't get lost. It tells them which direction is north, so they can find their way back home.

Airplane pilots and ship captains also use compasses so they don't get lost.

Magnetism is everywhere on this Earth of ours. It goes through air and water, glass and walls, cardboard and tabletops. You know this because your compass works just about everywhere. Try it and see for yourself. 🔹

**FOLLOW
UP**

What will you
need to collect
before you can
make a magnet
and a compass?
Would it be easier
to work with a
partner?

Understanding the Article

Magnets Attract

Reread the article. Then complete these sentences in your notebook.

- A magnet picks up only things that have a lot of ▭ in them.

- The whole Earth is a ▭, because it contains a lot of iron.

- The ends of your compass are called the north-seeking ▭ and the south-seeking pole.

- A compass points north because the ▭ is a magnet.

- When people go hiking, they take a ▭ so they won't get lost.

A Report

Write a short report about how you made a magnet, or how you made a compass. Explain how you found the materials you needed. Then tell what you did, step by step. Number the steps 1, 2, and so on. At the end, write a sentence or two explaining what you have learned.

TECH LINK
Use a computer to help you prepare your final draft.

Try It Yourself!

Work with a partner or two to try the activities in the article.

1. Start with the "fishing" activity. Collect the materials, then try it. What happens?

2. Make your own needle magnet. Remember to move it in one direction only. Does it pick up the same objects as your "fishing" magnet did?

3. Before you make your own compass, collect these things:

   • your needle magnet

   • two pieces of cork or foam plastic

   • a bowl of water

   • a marker pen

   Can you find the north-seeking end?

More Things to Try

Work with a family member to try these activities.

1. A refrigerator door has a magnet around it that holds the door tight. The magnet is under the plastic strip around the door. Test it with a paper clip. The door will hold the clip.

2. Take two bar magnets. Try placing them together, end to end. You'll find that sometimes the ends pull together, and sometimes they push away. Why? Because a north pole **attracts** a south pole, but two north poles or two south poles **repel** each other.

Science Fun

Hands-on Science with DR. ZED

Hot and Cold

Can you blow up a balloon without huffing and puffing?

HERE'S HOW

1. Remove the cap from an empty pop bottle and put the bottle in a freezer for fifteen minutes.

2. Blow up a small balloon to stretch it. Let the air out again.

3. Take the bottle out of the freezer, and pull the end of the balloon over the bottle opening.

4. Hold the bottle under your arm and watch the balloon pop up!

Elec-tricks

Your hair will stand on end when you try this trick! It works best on a dry day and with squeaky clean hair.

HERE'S HOW

1. Rub a blown-up balloon back and forth on your hair.

2. Look into a mirror and slowly pull the balloon away from your head.

3. Watch your hair rise!

4. Now hold the balloon against a wall. When you let it go, does the balloon stick to the wall?

*　*　*

Can a comb pick up paper? Yes!...If it's full of static electricity.

1. Run a plastic comb through your hair several times.

2. Hold the comb near small pieces of tissue paper or bits of paper towel.

3. Watch the paper jump!

You can make water wiggle without even touching it.

Turn on a cold water tap and let the water flow in a slow, steady stream. Then run a plastic comb through your hair. Hold the comb beside the stream of water. What happens to the water when you move the comb back and forth?

Watch the water wiggle!

Where will you do these activities? "Hot and Cold" would be easier at home. What about "Elec-tricks?" It would be fun if you could watch each other trying this in class!

Understanding the Science

Hot and Cold

- What happened when you did the experiment?
- Why do you think the balloon blows up when you warm the bottle?

Elec-tricks

Have you ever felt a spark after you walked across a carpet and touched something metal? That's because of static electricity.

- Why do you think a balloon can make your hair rise and stick to a wall?
- Why does the comb pick up paper?
- What else can you do with a comb using static electricity?

Look on the next page for Dr. Zed's answers!

Science TV

Look for fun science shows on TV. If you see one, come back and tell the class about it. Then everyone can watch the next episode.

Language Study

I DID IT YESTERDAY

How do you tell your family what you did in school each day? You use the **past tense**. What's that? Well, instead of saying, "I **learn** about static electricity," you would say, "I **learned** about static electricity." You change the verb **learn** from present to past. Usually, you add **-ed**, but not always.

In your notebook, write the sentences on the right. Fill in the spaces with the past tense of the verb in brackets. Remember, you're telling someone what you did yesterday. Check your answers with a partner.

1. Yesterday, I _____ (rub) a balloon on my hair.

2. Then I _____ (pull) the balloon away from my head.

3. My hair _____ (rise) up in the air!

4. Next, I _____ (run) a comb through my hair.

5. When I held the comb beside running water, the water _____ (wiggle).

Dr. Zed Explains

Hot and Cold

Cold air takes up less room than hot air. When you warm up the cold bottle with your body heat, the warm air expands (takes up more space). The expanding air has nowhere to go but into the balloon.

Elec-tricks

When you rub the balloon on your hair you make static electricity. The balloon can then stick to the wall and make your hair stand up. The comb picks up static electricity from your hair the same way. That's why it can pick up paper and attract the water, making it wiggle.

BEFORE READING

Read this page. Then look closely at the picture. Where do you see energy making things happen? Write your ideas in your notebook.

Many Kinds

Article by **Trudy Rising and Peter Williams**

Energy, energy, energy! What is it? It's what makes things happen. You are full of it. Energy makes you move. Your home is full of it. It makes lights glow and freezers freeze. It makes water flow and fires burn bright. The world is full of it. It makes flags flap, flowers bloom, trees sprout leaves. Without energy, nothing happens.

Energy comes in many different forms—**light, sound, motion, heat, electricity, chemistry, magnetism,** and more.

Take a close look at this picture. Can you find at least ten ways that energy is making things happen?

# of Energy

Light For Life

Our sun beams out huge amounts of energy all the time. How? The sun is a fiery hot ball of gas that keeps on exploding. These hot explosions produce solar energy that radiates into space.

Solar energy is energy that comes from the sun. This energy gives us light, keeps us warm, and lets us live. Only a tiny bit of the sun's energy reaches the Earth's surface. But what reaches us makes everything happen.

Solar Energy

Scientists are looking for better and cheaper ways to use solar energy. Some houses now have **solar cells** on the roof to help heat the house (see the picture on pages 68-69). Solar cells can supply power for flashlights, lighthouses, and space satellites.

Solar energy is a good way to create electricity. It's free and clean. Unlike fossil fuels (coal, oil, and gas), it doesn't pollute the air, it isn't dangerous to store, and it won't run out for millions of years.

Solar Surprise

Collect a few common objects, add sunshine, and watch the sun's energy cause something to happen.

What You'll Need

- bright sunlight
- a newspaper
- a few objects with different shapes: like kitchen tools, a pencil

What to Do

1. Place the newspaper in direct sunlight.

2. Put several objects on the newspaper.

3. Leave the newspaper in the sun for several hours.

What happened?

Wherever the sunlight hit the paper, it caused the paper to change colour. Why? Solar energy breaks down the dyes that colour the ink and the paper itself.

Blow Wind, Blow

Did you know the sun makes the wind? Here's how. When the sun shines, it heats up the air over an area of Earth. Because warm air is lighter than cold air, the warm air rises and cooler air moves in under it. Bingo! The moving air is wind.

Wind can be gentle or very strong. Its energy can bend trees, destroy homes, and even flip small airplanes off runways.

Wind Energy

In places where the wind blows constantly, people have found ways to put it to use. Instead of rows of crops, wind farms have rows of… yes, windmills!

Modern windmills, like those shown above, have blades shaped like an airplane's wing. The blades can swivel to use wind coming from any direction. The energy of the moving blades is used to generate electricity.

Your Own Wind

Now's your chance to prove you can make hot air. How? Use the heat of your hands to make your own wind.

What You'll Need

- paper and a pencil
- scissors
- an empty thread spool

What to Do

1. Trace the fan pattern onto your paper, then carefully cut it out. Make folds on the dotted lines.

2. Stick the eraser end of the pencil into the hole in the end of the spool.

3. Balance your fan on the pencil point. Be careful not to poke a hole in the paper fan.

4. Make sure your hands are warm. (If they're not, rub them together briskly.) Hold them, palms up, beneath the paper fan.

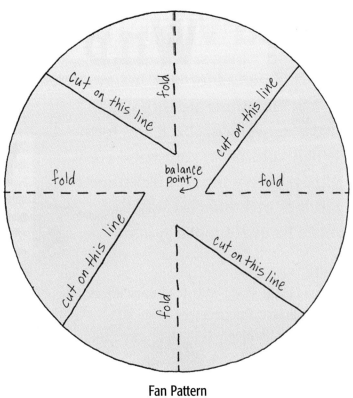

cut on this line   fold   cut on this line

fold   balance point   fold

cut on this line   fold   cut on this line

Fan Pattern

And Now

Watch what happens. Be careful not to touch the paper or the pencil. If your hands are warm enough, the fan will start to turn.

Good Vibrations

Sound is a form of energy caused by vibrations. Vibrations are very quick movements back and forth. When you speak, your vocal cords vibrate. Every musical instrument vibrates in a different way to make its own unique sound.

Flute
To make a flute sound, a player blows air across the mouth hole. This causes the air inside the flute to start vibrating.

Piano
Inside a piano are metal strings of various lengths. When you play the keys, little hammers hit the metal strings, which vibrate. The soundboard underneath the strings also vibrates to make the sound you hear.

Drum
A drum is made of a frame with a skin stretched over it. When the drummer taps the skin, the frame vibrates. These vibrations make the tapping sound bigger and longer.

Guitar
A guitar's sound is made when you pluck, pick, or strum the six strings, making them vibrate. The vibrations then bounce off the soundboard underneath the strings.

Create a Croaker

Here's your chance to make a musical instrument. It's called a croaker, probably because it sounds like...well, you'll see.

What You'll Need

- a small plastic yogurt container
- small scissors
- a piece of string 45 cm long
- a paper clip
- a cup of water

What to Do

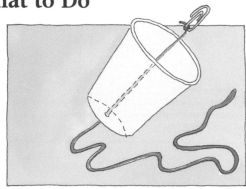

1. Cut a small hole in the centre of the bottom of the yogurt container. The hole should be just big enough for the piece of string to pass through.

2. Tie the paper clip to the end of the string so that it won't slip through the hole. Thread the string through the hole.

3. Hold the container in one hand. Dip the fingers of your other hand into the cup of water. Then slide your wet fingers down the string. Do this several times until you hear a sound. If you practise, you'll be able to make a better sound.

Sound Power

Even though you can't see sound, it can be very powerful. Recently, people in an apartment building thought they felt an earthquake. But it was only a rock group performing in a park nearby! What happened? The sound equipment created so many vibrations that the buildings started to sway.

What's happening?

The pull of your wet fingers causes vibrations in the string. The cup vibrates too, making the sound bigger. ◆

Now you can add to the list you made before reading. Look at the picture on pages 68-69 again. How many ways can you see energy working?

Congratulations! You're turning into a young scientist!

Understanding the Article

Energy Everywhere!

Work with a partner or a small group to answer these questions.

- How does the sun create energy?
- Why is solar energy a good way to create electricity?
- How do people use the energy of the wind?
- Do you think wind energy is a good way to create electricity?
- How do voices and musical instruments create sound?

Home Link Energy in Your Life

One form of energy in our homes is electricity. When you go home, look around you for all the ways you use electricity. Think about how often you use electricity every day. In your notebook, keep a record for one whole day of each time you use electricity. Ask your family members for help.

A Day Full of Energy

8:00 a.m.   I turn off my alarm clock.

8:01 a.m.   I turn on my light.

Try the Experiments!

Solar Surprise

- Try this experiment at home if you have a yard or balcony. Or ask if you can do it in the schoolyard.
- Did your experiment work the way you expected it to?

Your Own Wind

- Ask for help if you need it to cut out the windmill.
- Did your windmill move? Why do you think this works?

Create a Croaker

- The only tricky part is making the small hole to fit the string.
- How do you like the sound of your croaker?

 TECH LINK
What did you discover from these experiments? Share this knowledge with others on your school's Web site.

**B E F O R E
R E A D I N G**

Have you learned to ride a bicycle? Do you have your own bike? Where do you go when you ride it? What are the most important safety rules?

Bicycle Power

Article and Pictures by
Gail Gibbons

BICYCLE
(also called BIKE)

A bicycle is a two-wheeled vehicle that gets its power when the rider pushes the pedals around in a circle. The word **bicycle** means "two wheel." **Bi** means "two" and **cycle** means "wheel" or "circle."

The first idea for a bicycle was similar to this and is believed to have been drawn by the Italian artist and inventor, Leonardo da Vinci, about 500 years ago. His sketch looks a bit like the bicycles we see today.

The first bicycle was built in France about 1800. It didn't have pedals. Riders powered the **hobbyhorse** by using their feet to push along the ground in a running motion.

WOODEN WHEEL

CRANKS

VELOCIPEDE

IRON TIRE ON A WOODEN WHEEL

SOLID RUBBER TIRE ON A METAL WHEEL

HIGH-WHEELER (also called PENNY-FARTHING)

About 1840, the first bicycle with pedals was built. The pedals moved the rear wheel by using cranks. Next, a bicycle was invented that used pedals to power the bike by turning the front wheel. It was called the **velocipede**. About 1870, the **high-wheeler** (also called the **penny-farthing**) was built. It had a big front wheel that made it go faster.

Then about 1880, the first bicycle that looked like a modern bike was built. It was called the **safety bicycle**. The wheels on this bike were about the same size. Pedals moved the rear wheel by means of sprocket wheels and a chain.

1	SEAT
2	HANDLEBARS
3	FRAME
4	REFLECTORS
5	FRONT SPROCKET WHEEL
6	FRONT AXLE
7	FENDER
8	SPOKE
9	RIM
10	AIR-FILLED RUBBER TIRE
11	CRANK
12	PEDAL
13	KICKSTAND
14	REAR AXLE (inside hub)
15	REAR SPROCKET WHEEL
16	FOOT BRAKE (inside hub)
17	HUB

Today's bicycles are the result of many design changes. They are sturdier, safer, and lighter.

To give a bicycle its power, the rider pushes the pedals around and around. These pedals are attached to cranks that turn a sprocket wheel. The sprocket wheel is connected by the chain to a smaller sprocket wheel at the axle of the bicycle's rear wheel.

As the larger sprocket wheel turns, the rear sprocket wheel turns more quickly because it is smaller.

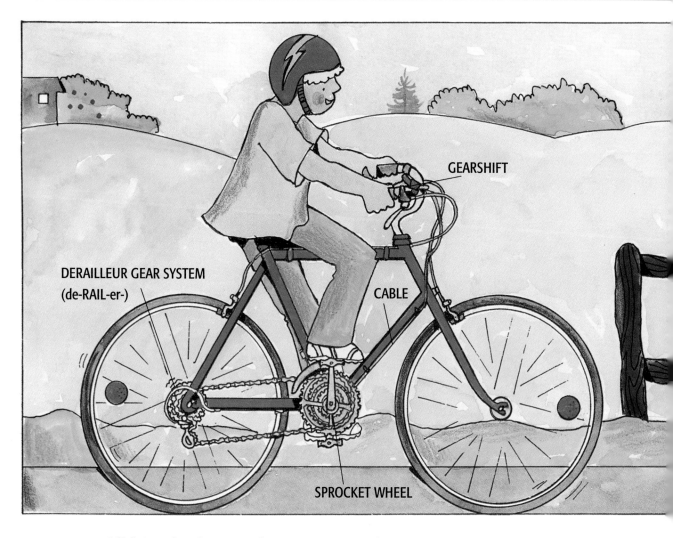

GEARSHIFT

DERAILLEUR GEAR SYSTEM
(de-RAIL-er-)

CABLE

SPROCKET WHEEL

All bicycles have at least two sprocket wheels, one at the pedals and one at the rear axle. When there are more than two sprocket wheels, there is a gear system. This makes pedalling easier at different times.
Many bikes have a derailleur* gear system that moves the chain from one sprocket wheel to another.
This happens when the rider moves the cable-operated gearshift.

Some bikes have an internal gear system at the rear wheel axle. The gears are shifted by moving the gearshift or twisting the handlebars.

*derailleur: a gadget that moves the chain from one gear to another

HANDLEBARS

GEARSHIFT

INTERNAL GEAR SYSTEM

AXLE

To steer a bike, turn the handlebars to make the front wheel turn. To stop, use either foot brakes or hand brakes. The foot brake stops a bike when one of the pedals is pushed backward. Each hand brake is connected to brake pads by a cable. When the hand lever is squeezed, the brake pads press against the rim of the wheel.

Biking is fun. You can go almost anywhere under your own power! ⬡

FOLLOW UP

What new things did you learn about bicycles from this article? Do you think bicycles are pretty complicated?

Understanding the Article

How Bikes Work

- Which of these historical bicycles would you like to try: the hobbyhorse, the velocipede, the high-wheeler, or the safety bicycle? Why?

- What happens when a rider pushes the pedals of a bicycle?

- Many bikes have a gear system. Why does changing gears make riding easier?

- What kind of energy makes a bicycle move? (**Hint**: A bike won't move without a rider!)

Compare the Diagrams to the Real Thing

Look at the picture of the basic bicycle on page 81. Look at the different parts of the bicycle. If possible, one student could bring a bicycle to class.

- Compare the real bicycle to the picture. Can you find all the labelled parts?

- Look at the other labelled pictures in the article. What kind of brakes does the real bike have? What kind of gearshift?

Illustrate Bicycle Safety Rules

Make a big poster called **Bicycle Safety**. On your poster, draw pictures illustrating each of these rules.
Add labels when you need them.
Can you think of three more rules?

1. Wear a bike helmet.

2. Obey traffic signs.

3. On bicycle trails, watch out for pedestrians.

4. Use hand signals for right turns, left turns, and stop or slow.

 TECH LINK
You could use a computer to help you draw or add labels to your poster.

Word Power

You've learned that **bi** means "two."
Here are some more words beginning with **bi**.
What do you think they mean?
Use your dictionary for help.

BI WORD	HINT	DEFINITION
bicuspid	a tooth	
biplane	a type of airplane	
biped	a type of animal	
biathlon	an Olympic sport	
biceps	a muscle	
bilingual	language	

Have you ever wondered how a TV show is made? Follow the process step by step as you read this article.

How a Chameleon Became a TV Star

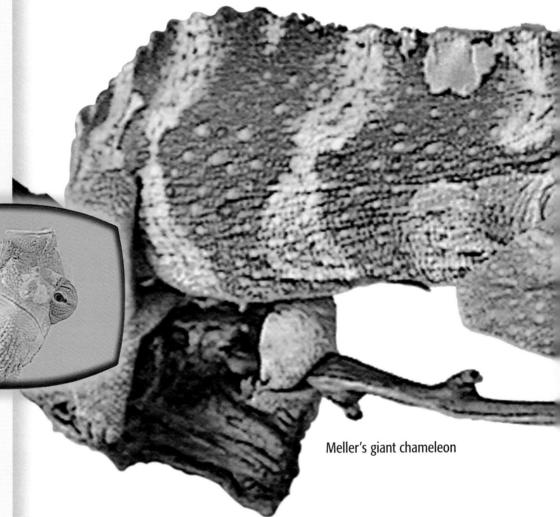

Meller's giant chameleon

Article by
Patricia Henderson

"Why do chameleons change colour?"
"Why does a snake shed its skin?"
"What's the biggest lizard in the world?"

KIDS@discovery is a television series that answers kids' questions about science. Let's take a look at how one half-hour show—called *Reptiles!*—is made!

How the Show Begins

The **producer** of the KIDS@discovery series is called Eva Everything. You won't see her on screen, but she's the boss in charge of almost everything. When Eva decides to do a show about lizards, snakes, turtles, crocodiles, and other reptiles, her team swings into action.

STEP #2

Looking Up Stuff

When a science show tells you something, it has to be true! That's where the **researcher**, Bree Tiffen, comes in. She knows how to find science experts around the world. For *Reptiles!*, she looks up herpetologists (scientists who study reptiles) on her computer. These scientists will help Bree make sure that all the facts on the show are correct.

STEP #3

Where to Find Reptiles

Reptiles don't hang around TV studios— you have to hunt for them! So Eva is excited when her team finds a great store nearby called Reptilia. It's full of healthy, happy reptiles. Reptile experts are on hand to explain things to visitors. Eva decides this is the perfect place to **videotape** a part of the show.

Teresa in front of Reptilia

Who Will Talk About the Reptiles?

James and Teresa

Eva meets with Teresa Roncon, the **host** of the show. The host is the person you see on screen, asking all the questions. (Teresa likes adventure, which is a good thing. On this show, she will have to hold a giant snake!) Eva and Teresa decide to interview two neat people at Reptilia. One is James Calderone, a thirteen-year-old reptile expert. He's been playing with reptiles since he was three. The other is Josh Feltham, a student of herpetology.

STEP #5

Preparing the Script

Teresa is not a scientist, but she is a curious person who wants to know about things. She writes down the questions she will ask the experts. This is called her **script**. Before doing her interviews, she learns the script so she won't have to read it in front of the camera.

Josh shows Teresa a turtle

Teresa tries on a corn snake

Out In the Field

Eva, Teresa, and the **camera operator**, Barry Smith, head out to Reptilia. Barry carries a very large video camera on his shoulder. He sets up lights where he needs them. Then he pins tiny microphones onto the experts' shirts so that their voices can be heard.

Filming the Show

Time to shoot! Eva holds a boa constrictor around her shoulders. It gives her a squeeze while she talks to James. He explains that the snake's backbone has three hundred vertebrae (little bones), making it super flexible. Later, they watch it grab a rat, squeeze hard, then gobble it up for dinner. Josh explains that a snake can swallow animals twice as big around as itself!

James and Teresa
with a boa constrictor

Starring... A Nervous Chameleon!

A **Meller's giant chameleon** lives at the Reptilia store. It's pale green, 25 cm long, and has a tongue twice as long as its body. Like all chameleons, it can change colour. When the camera operator turns on his lights, it gets so scared it turns black.

James and the other experts try to relax the chameleon. They know it won't show off its tongue unless it is calm. In the end, everyone has to wait for three hours until it feels like catching a fly. But it's worth it in the end. That long, grey, sticky tongue looks fantastic on TV!

Editing the Videotape

After eight hours at Reptilia, the TV crew has kilometres of videotape. Eva and the **editor**, Kevin McAuliffe, put the tape onto computer discs. Then they pick out the best shots and cut out the rest (this is called **editing**). They move the good shots around to make the show fast and lively. Some pictures will be on the screen for only four seconds!

Teresa, James, and snake expert Andy Beleny holding a Nile monitor

But There Were No Crocodiles at Reptilia!

When you see *Reptiles!* you will notice some pictures of crocodiles in Florida and iguanas on the Galapagos Islands. Bree found these shots in the videotape library at Discovery Channel. They get edited into the show along with the shots from Reptilia.

Iguanas on Galapagos Islands

Bits and Pieces

From time to time during the show, you'll see "DiscoveryBites." These are quick reptile facts. After you've read the words, they get swallowed by a hungry crocodile!

"Streeters" are neat, too. Barry goes out to meet some regular kids on the street and asks them a question, like "What is the world's biggest lizard?" Two of the kids know. Do you? (It's the Komodo dragon.)

Sound Effects

Sound effects are added last. After the boa constrictor eats the rat, you'll hear a giant burp! When the chameleon snaps out its tongue, you'll hear a noise like a whip. These sounds are just for fun. Finally, all the sounds and music get mixed in with the pictures. Whew! The show is finished!

Boa constrictor

Which Reptiles DO NOT Make Good Pets?

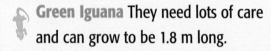 **Green Iguana** They need lots of care and can grow to be 1.8 m long.

Red-eared Slider Turtle These Asian turtles soon grow too big. If people release them into the wild, they compete for food with the native species of turtles.

Python One of these big snakes wrapped itself around its owner, who was trying to feed it. When a girl came to help, the snake wrapped her up too. Luckily, she was able to unwrap herself and then her friend. By that time, the owner was turning blue!

Meller's Giant Chameleon Sorry, this fellow is too easily scared to be a good pet.

Which Reptiles DO Make Great Pets?

Corn Snake Easy care—they only need feeding once every five days.

Bearded Dragon These lizards aren't too big, and they have little growths on their chins that pop out and turn black when they're angry.

Milk Snake These harmless snakes would make great bracelets! They have red, black, and white stripes around their bodies.

FOLLOW UP

Making a TV show is not simple! That's why the author explained things one step at a time.

Personal Response

- Have you ever kept a good (or not-so-good) reptile as a pet?
- What part of *Reptiles!* sounds most exciting to you?
- Do you think TV shows are a good way to learn about science?

Understanding the Article

Making a TV Show

How do each of these people help to make a science TV show?

- the producer
- the host
- the camera operator
- the sound effects person
- the researcher
- the science experts
- the editor

Which of these jobs would you most like to do?

Step-by-Step Instructions

Think of something that you know how to do well, like:

- **choosing a birthday present**
- **running a race**
- **playing a computer game**

Then write a set of step-by-step instructions. Explain how to do the activity to someone who has never done it.

Step 1:   The first thing you do is...

Step 2:   The next thing you do is...

Step 3:   When that's done, the next thing is...

Step 4:   One of the most important things is...

Design a Poster

Work with a small group of students. Choose a reptile pet you would like to keep at home. Find out how to feed and care for your pet.

Make a poster to display your information. Give it a BIG TITLE! Some group members can draw a big picture of the reptile pet. Others can make up a list of instructions on how to care for it.

Beginnings

So Will I

Poem by **Charlotte Zolotow**

My grandfather remembers long ago
the white Queen Anne's lace that grew wild.
He remembers the buttercups and goldenrod
from when he was a child.

He remembers long ago
the white snow falling falling.
He remembers the bluebird and thrush
at twilight
calling, calling.

He remembers long ago
the new moon in the summer sky.
He remembers the wind in the trees
and its long, rising sigh.
And so will I
         so will I.

How would you feel if you weren't allowed to read or write? That's how it was 150 years ago for nine-year-old Booker.

More Than Anything Else

Story by
Marie Bradby

Pictures by
Chris K. Soentpiet

Before light—while the stars still twinkle—Papa, my brother John, and I leave our cabin and take the main road out of town, headed to work.

The road hugs the ridge between the Kanawha River and the mountain. We travel it by lantern. My stomach rumbles, for we had no morning meal. But it isn't really a meal I want, though I would not turn one down.

More than anything else, I want to learn to read.

But for now, I must work. From sunup to sundown, we pack salt in barrels at the saltworks.

A white mountain of salt rises above Papa's head. All day long we shovel it, but it refuses to grow smaller.

We stop only to grab a bite—sweet potatoes and corn cakes that Papa has brought along in his coat pocket. As I eat every crumb of my meal, I stare at the white mountain. Salt is heavy and rough. The shiny white crystals leave cuts on your hands, your arms, your legs, the soles of your feet.

My arms ache from lifting the shovel, but I do not think about the pain there. I think about the hunger still in my head—reading. I have seen some people— young and old—do it. I am nine years old and I know, if I had a chance, I could do it, too.

I think there is a secret in those books.

In the chill of the evening, I follow Papa and John back up the road, stopping to catch a frog. The frog wiggles and slips, but I hold on tight and let go when I want to.

There is something different about this place where we live now. All people are free to go where they want and do what they can. Book learning swims freely around in my head and I hold it long as I want.

Back in town, coal miners, river men, loggers, and coopers gather on the corner. They are worn out as me, but full of tales.

I see a man reading a newspaper aloud and all doubt falls away. I have found hope, and it is as brown as me.

I see myself the man. And as I watch his eyes move across the paper, it is as if *I* know what the black marks mean, as if *I* am reading. As if everyone is listening to *me*. And I hold that thought in my hands.

I will work until I am the best reader in the county. Children will crowd around me, and I will teach *them* to read.

But Papa taps me on the shoulder. "Come on." And John tugs at my shirt. They don't see what I see. They don't see what I can be.

We hurry home. "Mama, I have to learn to read," I say. She holds my hand and feels my hunger racing fast as my heart.

It is a small book—a blue the colour of midnight. She gives it to me one evening in the corner of our cabin, pulling it from under the clothes that she washes and irons to make a little money.

She doesn't say where she got it. She can't read it herself. But she knows this is something called the alphabet. She thinks it is a sing-y kind of thing. A song on paper.

After work, even though my shoulders still ache and my legs are stained with salt, I study my book. I stare at the marks and try to imagine their song.

I draw the marks on the dirt floor and try to figure out what sounds they make, what story their picture tells.

But sometimes I feel I am trying to jump without legs. And my thoughts get slippery, and I can't keep up with what I want to be, and how good I will feel when I learn this magic, and how people will look up to me.

I can't catch the tune of what I see.
I get a salt-shovelling pain and feel my dreams
are slipping away.

I have got to find him—that newspaper man.

I look everywhere.

Finally, I find that brown face of hope.

He tells me the song—the sounds the marks make.

I jump up and down singing it. I shout and laugh
like when I was baptized in the creek. I have jumped
into another world and I am saved.

But I have to know more. "Tell me more," I say.

"What's your name?" he asks.

"Booker," I say.

And he takes the sound of my name and draws it on the ground.

I linger over that picture. I know I can hold it forever. ●

FOLLOW UP

Did Booker's story surprise you? Read "The Man Behind the Story" on this page to learn more about why things were so hard for him.

Hungry for Books

- What kind of work does Booker do with his father?
- Why does he want so badly to learn to read?
- Who does he meet who gives him hope?
- How does his mother help him?
- How does Booker learn to read in the end?

The Man Behind the Story

The boy in this story was a real person called Booker T. Washington. Booker was born a slave in Virginia in 1856. Slaves were not allowed to get an education, but Booker badly wanted to learn to read. Somehow his mother got him a spelling book so he could learn the alphabet.

Then everything changed. African Americans were freed from slavery after the Civil War. In 1865, a school opened in Booker's town, and he was allowed to attend for a few hours after work. Booker grew up to become an important teacher. He worked hard for a better future for African Americans.

North Star

Little Dipper

Big Dipper

The song "Follow the Drinking Gourd" told slaves to look for the Big Dipper, a group of stars.

Songs from the South

When they were slaves in the southern United States, African Americans sang wonderful songs. These "spirituals" gave them hope for a better life to come.

You may already know these songs:

"Swing Low, Sweet Chariot"

"Follow the Drinking Gourd"

Ask your teacher to help you learn some spirituals.

YOUR TURN TO WRITE

A Letter

What if you could write Booker a letter? What would you tell him about the present time? How would you encourage him to keep on learning? Write your letter. Share it with a partner.

Something To Think About

Reading was very important 150 years ago. There was no radio, no TV, and no Internet. To get information about many things, you had to read a book. Do you think reading is just as important today?

This article shows you how children might have lived more than 150 years ago. Of course, the photos are of modern children dressed up in pioneer clothes!

pioneers: people who are the first to explore and settle a new place

A Pioneer

Article by Bobbie Kalman *and* Tammy Everts

"Goodness, John, wake up. It's five o'clock already!" Mother called upstairs. John opened his eyes. Through the small window in his bedroom he could see that the sky was still dark. John stretched quickly and jumped out of bed—the morning chores had to be done.

When his feet hit the warm floor, he was thankful it wasn't winter. In winter he had to hop from foot to foot to keep his toes from freezing. The water in his washbowl would be so cold that a thin layer of ice floated on the top!

Child's Day

After dressing in his cotton shirt and comfortable trousers, John hurried downstairs and rushed out to the barn to join his father.

John's home does not have a sink or plumbing. Instead, John keeps a pitcher of water and a washbowl in his bedroom for washing his face and hands in the morning.

Morning chores

Together, Father and John milked the cows, cleaned the calf pens, and fed the livestock. After giving his pet calf a quick pat, John returned to the house for breakfast.

A hearty breakfast

In the kitchen, Mother and sister Emily bustled around the fireplace preparing breakfast. Soon Father came in, and the family sat down to a hearty breakfast of sizzling bacon, fried potatoes, hot buckwheat pancakes with sweet maple syrup, fresh bread and preserves, and doughnuts.

John takes a moment to pet his cow, Daisy. Daisy wonders if John has a tasty treat hidden in his hand.

Time for school

John and Emily took the lunch box that their mother had prepared for them and walked the half-hour trek to school. There was a spelling bee that day, and Emily's team won, as usual. No one could spell as well as Emily. John was happy when the day was over because he hated to see Emily gloat!

John and Emily "horse around" on the family wagon. Giddyup!

Chores and dinner

After school, John enjoyed helping Father care for the animals. He spread fresh hay in the stalls of the cows, oxen, calves, pigs, and sheep so the animals could have soft, clean beds. He fed the animals and milked the cows. Finally, it was time for dinner.

Children did adult work such as caring for the oxen.

Happy evenings by the fire

After dinner, Mother and Emily washed the dishes and cleaned the kitchen. Father sat by the fireplace and whittled a new handle for his axe. John played with some building blocks his father had made for him.

Evenings were a happy time when the family sat together around the fire and ate apples, beechnuts, and popcorn. At nine o'clock, everyone went to bed. They needed plenty of rest for the next busy day.

A full, busy life

Early pioneer children had lives that were very different from those of boys and girls today. Difficult work was a part of every day. In order to have enough food and clothing, the entire family had to work hard. Boys and girls began to do chores as soon as they were able to walk and talk. Parents loved their children, but they were very strict. They had to be—a family needed co-operation and teamwork to get everything done.

Emily helps her mother spin thread, weave cloth, make candles, and sew clothing. In those days children learned how to sew when they were young. By the time she was four years old, Emily had already stitched her first quilt square!

Using their imagination

Even though boys and girls worked hard, they always found time for fun. Many children today have a huge variety of toys, games, and activities from which to choose. Pioneer children had to amuse themselves with simple games and a few homemade toys. Most of these games were played outdoors, using objects found around the farm or in the community. An old barrel hoop provided hours of fun when it was rolled with a stick. With a bit of pretending, a fence could be a bucking horse to ride. A sturdy board laid over a tree stump became a simple seesaw. Rocks, leaves, and branches created imaginary houses and forts. A child's only limit was his or her imagination.

Not every minute was devoted to work. Children played with simple but fun toys.

With a partner, discuss how your life is different from John and Emily's. How would you describe the life of a pioneer child?

Understanding the Article

A Pioneer's Life

- What chores did John and Emily do on the farm?
- Why did pioneer children have to work?
- What games did pioneer children play?
- How was school different for pioneer children?
- Do you think pioneer children had a difficult life or not? Why?

Invent a Game

Pioneer children had no TV or computer games. To amuse themselves, they invented games and made their own toys. You can do the same! Invent a game you and your friends could play outside, using only simple objects.

Make a poster to show how your game is played.

1. Give the game a title.
2. Draw a picture that shows kids playing the game.
3. Add instructions on how to play the game.

Interview an Older Friend

Do you have grandparents or older friends living nearby? Interview them about life when they were children.

- In your notebook, list ten questions to ask your older friend. For example:

  Did they ever win a spelling bee?

  What did they do for fun?

- Set up a time for the interview. Ask your questions.

- Write down the answers in your notebook.

- Share what you learn with the class.

TECH LINK
You could share this interview by posting it on your school's Web site.

WRITING IN YOUR JOURNAL

In your notebook, make a list of jobs that you do at home and at school. How do you feel about helping out? What other jobs could you do to help?

Begin Again!

Poems collected by
David Booth

Pictures by
Maryann Kovalski

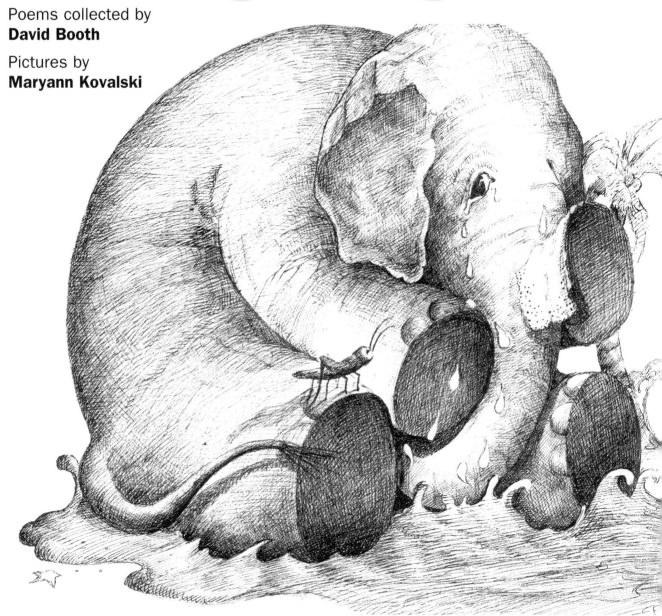

Way down south where bananas grow,
A grasshopper stepped on an elephant's toe.
The elephant said, with tears in his eyes,
"Pick on somebody your own size."

How much wood would
a woodchuck chuck
If a woodchuck could
chuck wood?

I eat my peas with honey.
I've done it all my life.
It makes the peas taste funny.
But they sure stick on the knife.

There was a man called Michael Finigan,
He grew whiskers on his chinigin,
The sun came out and drove them in ag'in.
Poor old Michael Finigan, begin ag'in.

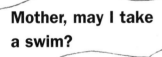

Mother, may I take
a swim?

Yes, my darling daughter,
But hang your clothes on
a hickory limb,
And don't go near the water.

If Peter Piper picked a
peck of pickled peppers,
Where's the peck
of pickled peppers
Peter Piper picked?

Personal Response

- Which of these rhymes is the funniest? What makes it funny?
- Memorize your favourite rhyme and repeat it at home.

Rhyme Collection

Home Link

Ask your parents or other family members what rhymes they remember from when they were young. Write these rhymes down. Draw a picture for each rhyme. Start a class collection of rhymes.

BEFORE READING

Read the title of this story. What do you think a silk train is? Do you think Emma will go on a train trip in this story?

Emma
and the
Silk Train

Story by *Julie Lawson*
Pictures by *Paul Mombourquette*

"Silker's coming!"

Emma ran to join her brother Charlie, drawn by the wail of the whistle, the billowing smoke, and the rhythm of wheels rolling over the rails.

"Not so close!" Mama shouted from the station window.

Charlie grabbed Emma's hand and pulled her back.

Emma didn't mind. She was still close enough to feel the ground tremble as the silk train thundered past.

Emma's pa ran the station, so she knew all the trains. The only ones she cared about were the silkers—because hidden inside was a precious cargo of silk.

Pa said the silk came over the ocean all the way from China. It was so valuable, silk trains rushed it across the country to New York, stopping only long enough to change crews and hook up a fresh engine with a full head of steam. Regular trains had to wait while the silkers sped through. Once, even a royal train was moved aside for a silker.

When Emma was five, Mama had fashioned a silk blouse for herself. Emma loved how it shimmered. There was enough silk left over for a hair ribbon for Emma and two squares for her patchwork quilt. But from that moment on, Emma longed for a silk blouse of her own.

One day, Emma came home from school to find the station in an uproar.

"There's been an accident," Pa explained. "A silker's derailed. Five cars are in the river. One broke open, and bales of silk are floating downstream."

"And there's a reward!" Charlie rubbed his hands gleefully. "The railroad's paying five dollars for every bale fished out of the river!"

Emma's mind reeled. Maybe she'd find some, enough for another hair ribbon—or even a blouse, like Mama's.

The next morning, the whole town was fishing for silk.

By the end of the day, everyone had caught something.

A few people caught bales of raw silk.

Charlie caught a salmon.

Pa caught his fly-fishing hat, the one the wind had blown away the month before.

Mama caught a cold.

And Emma caught silk-fishing fever.

Long after everyone else had stopped, Emma kept fishing.

Sometimes she fished from shore.

All she caught was a gumboot.

Sometimes she fished from the wharf.

All she caught was a rusty kettle.

Sometimes she fished from the rowboat.

All she caught was disappointment.

"No more boat rides," Charlie decided one day. "Sorry, Emma, but it's been two weeks since the last silk bale was found."

But Emma didn't give up easily.

She searched the river bank, in places where bales might be trapped by roots or partly buried in sand.

Still she found nothing.

One afternoon, Emma's search took her farther than she was allowed to go. She was rounding the bend, promising herself she would head straight back, when she saw a splash of colour a little ways from shore. The current caught the colour and unfolded it into one long rippling stream. It looked red, until the sunlight touched it. Then it shimmered gold.

"Silk!" Emma cried. Enough for a blouse like Mama's—or even a dress! Quickly, she pulled off her shoes and stockings and hitched up her skirt. Bracing herself against the cold, she waded into the river.

The water licked at the hem of her skirt and swirled around her knees.

Just a few more steps—

Emma reached out and grabbed her prize.

Triumphant, Emma turned to go back. But at that moment the current tugged on the silk. Determined to hold on, Emma lost her balance. She gasped in panic as the river swept her off her feet.

Emma clutched the silk in her hand. She wouldn't let go. Not now! Gritting her teeth, she swam hard to reach the river bank.

But she was no match for the current as it carried her farther and farther downstream.

Up ahead, Emma spotted a small island. Desperately, she fought the current as it threatened to pull her past.

She tried to touch bottom. Once, twice—

On her third try her toes grazed against something. Then her foot hit the muddy bottom.

She staggered to shore and collapsed in the sand.

She had made it. And she still had her silk.

But as Emma looked at the fast-flowing water between her and the distant river bank, she began to feel uneasy. How would she get off the island?

Wet and cold, Emma huddled against a log.

She scanned the river bank, hoping to see someone, straining to hear a voice.

Silence. The bank was deserted.

The sun crept lower in the sky. Long shadows played tricks, making bushes and branches look like people waving from shore and walking along the tracks.

Tracks! The thought of them gave Emma an idea.

Standing on the log, she tied her silk so it flowed like a banner between two trees.

Then she waited.

Shadows grew longer. The silk snapped in the rising wind.

Emma rubbed her arms and stamped her feet to keep warm.

In the distance she heard a low, shaky rumble that swelled to a locomotive roar. A train burst around the curve. A silker!

Emma jumped up and down, waving frantically. "Help!" she shouted. "It's me, Emma! STOP!"

But the train thundered past, vanishing in a cloud of flying cinders.

Emma swallowed hard. Silkers never stopped. Not for regulars, not for royalty, not for her.

The train's wailing whistle faded away, lost in the rush of the river, the sweep of the wind.

Emma waited. The sky turned black. One star appeared.

A westbound freight came into sight. Emma leaped to her feet and waved, but the train rumbled past.

A sob caught in her throat. What if no one finds me? she thought fearfully. What if I'm here all night, all alone?

She shuddered.

Then she heard it. Faintly at first, but growing steadily stronger. Voices calling. "EM-MA! EM-MA!"

Light flickered over the water.

"Mama!" she cried. "Pa! I'm here!"

Behind her, the silk caught the light and shone.

"Emma! Are you all right?" Mama hurried out of the rowboat and swept Emma into her arms. "We were so worried!"

"Oh, Mama!" Emma burst into tears. "I was afraid you'd never find me."

Mama wrapped Emma snugly in a blanket and wiped away her tears. "Thank heavens the crew on the silker spotted that banner you made. As soon as the train reached the station, the fireman swung down from the steps—"

"The silker *stopped*?" Emma was amazed.

Mama chuckled. "Not completely. Just slowed down enough for the fireman to hand your pa the message."

They were getting into the boat when Emma looked over her shoulder. "Where's my silk?" she cried out in alarm.

"Right here," Charlie said, placing it in her outstretched hands. "Boy, Emma. This is some catch."

As Charlie rowed to shore, Mama turned to Emma and scolded gently. "You got a little carried away, fishing for silk. You know you're not to go past the bend."

Emma nodded. "I'm sorry, Mama." She snuggled closer as Mama stroked her hair. "Will it be all right?" she asked.

Mama gave her a hug. "Now that you're safe and sound? Of course."

"I meant—"

"And the silk will be grand, you'll see."

Emma's birthday came three weeks later.

Charlie eyed the cake hungrily. "Hurry up, Emma. Make a wish."

"Listen!" she whispered. "Silker's coming!"

A circle of light burst through the darkness. The whistle wailed as the train roared past the station.

Emma smiled. She didn't need to make a wish. Her new silk dress rustled as she leaned forward to blow out the candles.

Were you surprised to find out what a silk train was? What did you think of Emma's adventures?

Congratulations! You've boarded the good reader's train!

Understanding the Story

Silker's Coming!

- Why does Emma know all about trains?
- Why is everyone so excited when the silk train derails?
- How does Emma get into trouble fishing for silk?
- How does she try to get the attention of the passing silk train?
- Why doesn't Emma make a wish when she blows out her birthday candles?

Find Out More About...

Do you know how silk is made? What is a silkworm? Write down three things that you learned about silk from this story. Now write down three questions you still have. With a partner, research silk and silkworms to find out how silk is made. Share this information with your class.

TECH LINK
Check the Internet for information on silk and silkworms.

Silkworm cocoon

WRITING IN YOUR JOURNAL

Have you ever taken a train trip? Where did you go? How did you feel? Describe what you saw, what you heard, and what you smelled. If you have never been on a train, imagine what it would be like!

Read about author Julie Lawson on page 124.

Did You Know ?

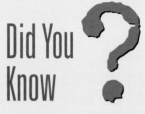

The silk trains set records for speed. Why did they travel so fast? The quicker the journey, the more money the silk owners made. Also, the trains carried cocoons of live silkworms. A long journey could be dangerous for them. Silk trains disappeared when the Panama Canal opened, and silk was sent by ship instead.

Silkworm moth

Woman in silk dress making silk from cocoons

MEET AUTHOR

Julie Lawson

Interview by Susan Hughes

Susan: When did you first become interested in writing stories?

Julie: I began writing stories when I was in grade three. I loved reading, too. I read fairy tales, legends, and myths. When I got older, I loved reading historical fiction (stories about the old days), and adventure stories.

Susan: How did you find out about silk trains?

Julie: I've always been interested in trains. My grandfather worked for the Canadian Pacific Railway (CPR). He told many stories about trains to my mother—and she passed them along to me.

Then, one evening I was listening to the radio. I heard someone speaking about a real event. A silk train had derailed along the Fraser River in British Columbia in 1927. Bales of silk had gone floating downstream. This sparked my interest right away! I did lots of research and learned all about it. You know, I didn't realize it until I began writing *Emma and the Silk Train*, but I was already connected to this event!

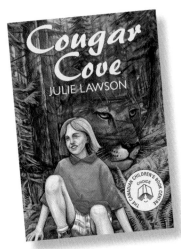

Susan: What do you mean?

Julie: I had completely forgotten that my grandfather had been given a length of silk from the CPR one Christmas. My grandmother turned it into a dress, but there were scraps left over. One birthday, when I was a child, she gave me a dress for my doll. It was made from these scraps of silk!

When I began researching the silk trains, I suddenly remembered this dress. I remembered how I loved it, how it rustled, how the light shone on it.

Susan: How did you turn the silk train accident into a story?

Julie: I began using the "What if?" magic! I learned that the CPR offered rewards for the return of the bales of silk. People began fishing in the river for the bales. I wondered, what if one child gets carried away in this search? What if she goes a little bit farther than she is supposed to? What if she races to catch a bale of silk and the river knocks her off her feet? The author in me wanted to put her in a really tricky situation—and see how she was going to get out!

Susan: Do you have any tips for young writers?

Julie: Read as much as you can. Do a lot of writing. And always be aware of possibilities. Take a look around your own room. Take a fresh look at something you might see every day. Now put in some magic. Ask "What if?" and "What could happen?" You can make new beginnings happen! ●

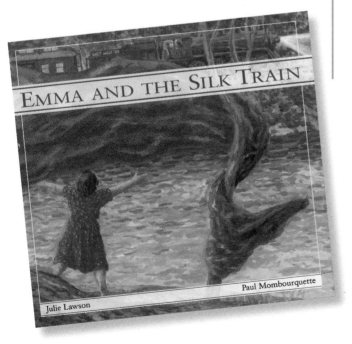

EMMA AND THE SILK TRAIN

Julie Lawson

Paul Mombourquette

Make a Balancing Acrobat

Do you know what kinds of toys pioneer children played with? These instructions explain how to make one kind of pioneer toy.

ACTIVITY BY **Barbara Greenwood**
PICTURES BY **Heather Collins**

Early settlers had little time for fun in their busy days. But in the evenings, as they sat before the fire, out would come a jackknife to carve a wooden animal or make a clever toy, like this balancing acrobat.

You will need

a round toothpick
a bottle cork
markers
two skewers or knitting needles
modelling clay
a piece of string 1 m long

1 Break a toothpick in half. Push the pointed end into the centre of one end of the cork. Let it stick out about 2.5 cm. Ask an adult to make a notch in the end with a knife. This is the pivot.

2 Use markers to draw a face and clothes on the cork acrobat.

3 Stick the skewers into the sides of the cork at an angle, as shown. The angles must be the same.

4 Shape the clay into two balls, each about 2.5 cm in diameter. They must be the same size. Stick them onto the ends of the skewers.

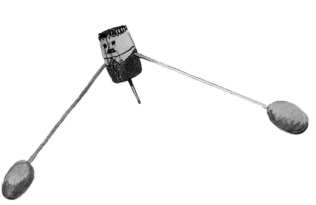

5 Balance the acrobat on the tip of one finger by its pivot. If it falls off, it is not evenly weighted. Try adjusting the angle of the skewers or evening up the size of the balls.

6 Ask two friends to hold the string tight. Balance the acrobat on the string. Raise or lower one end of the string to make the acrobat "walk." ●

Make a Balancing Acrobat **127**

FOLLOW UP

Do you think it will be easy or hard to make the balancing acrobat? How do you think it will turn out?

Crafty Words

What do the numbered words below mean? In your notebook, write the number of each word. Match it with the letter of the correct definition and diagram on the right.

For example: 1. = e)

1. skewer

a) a line through the centre of a ball

2. diameter

b) a point that something turns or moves on

3. pivot

c) two lines that meet and the space between them

4. angle

d) loaded with weights

5. notch

e) a long wooden or metal pin

6. weighted

f) a V-shaped cut

Craft Show

What types of crafts do you and your classmates enjoy making? Hold a craft show to display the work of your class. Make some new crafts and bring in crafts you've already made. Invite family members and other classes to come and see your crafts. Explain to your guests how the crafts were made.

IMAGINE!

What if you made a balancing acrobat and it came to life? Tell the story of what happens.

Try It Yourself

- ✏ Before you begin making the acrobat, collect everything you're going to need.
- ✏ Read the instructions. Are there any you don't understand?
- ✏ Follow the steps carefully to make the balancing acrobat.

- ✏ Draw a special face on the cork—your creation!
- ✏ Show others how your balancing acrobat was made and how it works.

Do you have a special place? Who took you there? How does it make you feel?

Noon on the Mountain

Story by **Jan Bourdeau Waboose**   Pictures by **Karen Reczuch**

Mishomis: grandfather

Noshen: grandson

Grandfather is looking up. I know he is searching the sky. Grandfather is wise and knows many things. He says I will too.

"When, Mishomis?" I ask.

"In time," he answers. "Wisdom will come."

I stand beside Grandfather. I look up and search too. The sun is low on the horizon. I feel the wind's wings, warm on my arms and legs.

Grandfather speaks softly. "It is time—we will go."

I want to jump up and down and make a lot of noise. But I do not. For where we are going only silence is needed. We leave before the sun climbs to the centre of the sky.

I follow Grandfather like a shadow. Quietly, quickly, he moves like a fox, over the familiar path of the forest floor. I know that many animals have made this trail as they walked beneath the ancient white pines that whisper and past the singing water of the river.

But I don't see any of them today, only Grandfather ahead of me. I try to stay close behind, but it is not easy keeping up with his strong, silent strides. I stop a moment to taste a plump purple berry from a saskatoon bush and then hurry on.

I am hot and thirsty. There are beads of sweat on my nose. I am getting tired but I do not slow down.

Finally Grandfather stops. We are almost there. Almost. He turns to me and smiles. "You travel swiftly with soft steps. That is good. Now you must show strength as well."

He points to a rocky cliff and then tousles my hair with his long fingers. His dark brown eyes are bright and catch the sun's reflection.

"Are you ready, Noshen?"

I wipe the sweat from my nose, take a deep breath and nod.

"I am, Mishomis."

Before we begin our climb, I watch my grandfather's strong brown arms reach out and spread open to the turquoise sky. So I too stretch my arms high. Grandfather looks at me and nods.

As I climb, I can feel each rough groove etched in the face of the cliff. Its surface is hot and dry under my sweaty palms. My fingers are red and tingling, and I feel the hard ridges of rock pressing against my bare knees.

The cliff is steep, so I avoid looking down. Although I am not afraid, I am tiring. I keep up with Grandfather, but my legs feel as heavy as rocks. I cannot let this slow me, for I know that many ancestors have climbed here before me, and before Grandfather too. I imagine each foothold, formed through time by their steps.

Finally, we reach the top. The sun is high. It is very still and quiet.

I can look back now, but as I turn, I notice a large shadow cast down on the ground. I quickly look up but cannot see what has made the shadow. Instead, I see thin birch trees waving in the soft breeze. It is strange because I cannot hear the leaves rustling. Neither can I feel the wind cooling my skin or smell the dry moss under my moccasins.

Up here, I stand closer to the noon sun, yet I do not feel the heat, nor do I have to shield my eyes from its brightness.

Grandfather sits down and motions for me to sit beside him. I do. He does not speak. Neither will I. This is his special place. Noon is his favourite time, and so it is mine.

We look out over the fast-flowing river and the thick green forest below. I can see with birds' eyes. I feel that I am soaring, touching the endless sky, floating through powder-white clouds. Flying free, high above our world.

Very still, we wait, perched on top of our rocky nest. I can hear my own breathing. It is loud. I cannot hear Grandfather's. I wonder if he is holding his breath. I want to look at him, take one quick peek. But then... I see a powerful bird in slow motion. Alone and gliding.

In silence he moves with smooth graceful strokes. Around and around, he circles us with wings reaching like Mother's arms. Motionless, we watch.

The Great Eagle.

Suddenly, the eagle is looking at me. He is coming in my direction. Faster and closer he flies.

I do not move, not one part of my body. Oh, how I want to hold on to Grandfather. But I do not. My heart is pounding like the beat of the drum.

And then the eagle swoops down. I can hear the rapid rhythm of strong wings. I want to squeeze my eyes shut, but I keep them open, watching. He is here. His scent fills my nostrils. I feel talons combing through my hair with a gentleness I cannot explain.

Then he is gone, as swiftly as he appeared.

I let out a long breath and look at Grandfather. He is smiling, a very big smile. He points to the ground. There before us lies a long soft eagle feather.

I feel Grandfather's warm strong hands holding my shoulders as he speaks.

"Noshen, our people see the eagle as a powerful messenger. His presence is a sign of honour and wisdom. As the Great Eagle is a proud protector of our people, I am a proud Mishomis of my Noshen."

And so, I too am proud, just like Grandfather.

FOLLOW UP

What is Grandfather's special place? Do you think you would like this place, too?

Understanding the Story

A Special Place

- Why do the boy and his grandfather walk and climb so silently?

- How does the boy know that his ancestors have walked the trail before him?

- What magical thing happens to the boy on the cliff top?

- How does Grandfather explain the eagle's message?

- What new beginnings will the boy have after this experience?

About the Author and the Artist

The author, Jan Bourdeau Waboose, grew up in northern Ontario. She lived both on and off the Ojibway reserve. Her writing shows how she loves nature and her people's traditions.

The illustrator, Karen Reczuch, also loves the wilderness. She has been canoeing in the north for over twenty years.

WRITER'S CRAFT

Similes

A **simile** uses the words **like** or **as** to compare different things. For example, Jan Bourdeau Waboose compares a heart to a drum:

> "My heart is pounding like the beat of the drum."

In your notebook, finish these sentences with a simile:

> I'm so tired my muscles feel like...
>
> Far below, the birches look like...
>
> The cliff is as high as...

Try writing more similes of your own.

A Personal Story

Write about a place in nature that's special to you. It could be out in the country or in a city park. Do you sometimes meet birds or animals there? Describe what you see, hear, smell, and feel.

TIP › Remember to use similes.

MORE GOOD READING

When Bear Stole Chinook
A Siksika Tale
by Harriet Peck Taylor

A young boy is helped by his animal friends as he tries to trick Bear into giving back the warm winds of spring.
(a picture book folk tale)

🍁 **Tess**
by Hazel Hutchins

Tess loves living on the prairie and riding her horse, Chinook. But it's a hard, hungry life for her and her parents.
(a picture book story)

🍁 **The Always Prayer Shawl**
by Sheldon Oberman

When Adam comes from Russia to Canada, he brings a precious family heirloom that he'll hand on to his grandson one day.
(a picture book story)

🍁 **Tides of Change: Faces of the Northwest Coast**
by Sheryl McFarlane

With poetry and beautiful pictures, this book tells some of the history of British Columbia.
(a picture book poem)

Just the Facts

Just the Facts

◆

A calendar is a good way to keep track of birthdays and other special days. On this calendar, you'll read about festivals that happen every month of the year!

Festival Calendar

JANUARY

Sun Nin, the Chinese New Year

This celebration starts in January, but ends in February. For a whole month, Chinese families spend time together and celebrate the new year, sharing a huge feast on New Year's Eve. In Vancouver and many other cities, a huge dragon dances through the streets on the last day.

Iroquois Midwinter Festival

At this eight-day festival, the Iroquois celebrate the new year and pray to the Creator. Two special dances are the Feather Dance and the Skin Dance.

F E B R U A R Y

Festival of the Voyageurs

In St. Boniface, Manitoba, people celebrate the fur traders of long ago. See their canoes, visit a trapper's cabin, and enjoy pea soup!

Québec City's Winter Carnival

A jolly snowman— *Bonhomme Carnaval*— welcomes you to Québec City! Enjoy the winter sports and the wonderful ice sculptures.

M A R C H

Sugaring-Off

When the sap starts running in the trees, it's time to make maple syrup. In Québec, people enjoy maple syrup feasts—ham, omelettes, pancakes stuffed with bacon, and maple syrup— in the sugar shack!

Spring Equinox

This is one of only two days when daylight and darkness are equal—twelve hours each. (The other day is the Autumn Equinox.) Many people celebrate the longer days and the coming of spring.

141

APRIL

Toonik Tyme

Inuit legends tell of Toonik, a giant man. In Iqaluit, Nunavut, the Inuit honour him with hilarious competitions—tugs-of-war on ice, the Backwards Parka Race, and many other fun and traditional games.

April Fool's Day

This is the day when people tell jokes and play tricks on each other. So watch out!

MAY

Victoria Day

Canadians celebrate Queen Victoria's birthday with a long weekend. This is the time to plant your garden—winter is really over!

Mother's Day

What do you do on Mother's Day to show your mom how special she is? In Alberta, some First Nations groups have a special dance in honour of Mother's Day. This dance is part of a big spring pow-wow.

JUNE

Midsummer's Eve

For many people from Europe, June 23 is a special time. Summer holidays are just around the corner.

Father's Day

The third Sunday in June is a special day for honouring Dads.

JULY

Canada Day

July 1 is Canada's birthday. Thousands of people celebrate in Ottawa, but contests and fireworks light up the whole country.

Pile O'Bones Sunday

The City of Regina, Saskatchewan, sits on land that was once called Pile O'Bones, because Plains First Nations hunters left a pile of buffalo bones there. Every year a large picnic is held in Regina on the last Sunday in July. The picnic includes a Buffalo Days costume contest, and lots of good food.

AUGUST

Caribana

Caribbean Canadians hold a huge parade in Toronto. Adults and children wear fantastic costumes and dance to steel band music.

Scottish Highland Games

People show off their dancing skills, and toss the caber (like a telephone pole!). Listen for the bagpipes!

S E P T E M B E R

Fall Fairs

Small towns across Canada celebrate the harvest throughout the fall. Watch for barbecues, sweet corn, midway rides, and much more.

Labour Day

It's the last long weekend before school starts. This holiday began a hundred years ago with a parade to support workers.

O C T O B E R

Thanksgiving

Families give thanks for the harvest and share a special dinner—turkey, cranberry sauce, and pumpkin pie. Yum!

Halloween

Carve the pumpkins and stock up on candies! Here come the kids in their costumes.

NOVEMBER

Remembrance Day

On November 11, Canadians remember the soldiers who died for their country in World War I (1914-1918) and World War II (1939-1945).

Divali

The Hindu festival of lights began in India. People light little clay lamps in honour of Lakshmi, the goddess of good fortune.

DECEMBER

Christmas

This Christian festival celebrates the birth of Jesus. Kids help to decorate an evergreen tree, give and receive gifts, and sing special carols.

On Christmas Eve, Cree children in the James Bay area visit relatives. At each home, they are given a cloth sack to hang up. On Christmas Day, they go visiting again and collect their bags—now full of presents!

Chanukah (also Hanukkah)

During this Jewish festival of lights, children light candles, sing songs, and play with a special top called a *dreydel*.

How many of
these festivals have
you celebrated?

**Personal
Response**

• What's your favourite
festival of the year?
• What festivals would you
add to the Festival Calendar?
• Choose a festival you'd like to celebrate with your
classmates this year.

More Good Reading
Find out more about how
Canadians celebrate by
reading *Let's Celebrate*
by Caroline Parry.

Home Link

Make Your Own Calendar

Think about your favourite things to do
each year—your birthday, summer holidays,
visits to relatives, school sports days, and
anything else you enjoy. On a large sheet
of paper, draw twelve boxes. In the boxes,
write in the names of the months.
For each month, write a sentence about
your favourite thing to do. Then illustrate
each box with pictures.

   Share your calendar with family
members and ask them to add things
they like to do. Each family member
could use a different colour.

Peace Projects

The International Day of Peace falls on September 16th. But peace can be celebrated any day. Here are two ideas to try at school:

- Make a peace chain. Everyone in your school makes a wish for peace and writes it on one link of a paper chain. Join the links and chains together. Hang the peace chain along the hallway or around the gym.

- Write a message of peace on your school's Web site.

Get together with a small group. Invent your own ideas for celebrating peace. Choose a special Peace Day to do your activities.

Festival Quiz

In your notebook, write the name of the festival where you could do each of these things:

- spin a dreydel
- have a tug-of-war
- enjoy the fireworks
- eat corn on the cob
- dance to steel band music
- judge the ice sculptures

Just the Facts

Rice Squares

Recipe by *Caroline Parry*

People from Southeast Asia celebrate the New Year in mid-April, when spring is bringing the world back to life. Rice squares are a favourite New Year's festival treat. This tasty recipe comes from Sri Lanka.

KITCHEN TOOLS

measuring cups
measuring spoons
a saucepan with cover
a strainer
a bowl
a wooden spoon
a 2 L cake pan (8-inch-square)

INGREDIENTS

125 mL	white rice	1/2 cup
375 mL	water	1 1/2 cups
125 mL	flaked coconut	1/2 cup
30 mL	sugar	2 tbsp

DIRECTIONS

1. Rinse the rice in a strainer, then put it into a saucepan.
2. Pour the water over the rice and cover the pan. Bring the rice and water to a boil over HIGH heat. Turn the heat down to LOW. Cook for about 8 minutes until the rice is tender (it will look soupy).
3. Place the rice in a strainer and let the water drip into a bowl. Pour this leftover water into a measuring cup. Add enough cold water to make 250 mL (1 cup).
4. Put the water and the rice back into the pan. Add the coconut and sugar. Stir. Cook and stir over LOW heat until all the water is gone.
5. Pour the mixture into the cake pan. Smooth it out with a spoon and let it cool for 20 minutes. Chill in the refrigerator for one more hour.
6. Cut into squares. Top each rice square with a little jam or honey.

Caution: Only use the stove with an adult present.

SHARING RECIPES

Do you have a favourite family festival recipe? Print it out clearly on a card. Bring your recipe to class and put it in a box. Let everyone pick a recipe. Take it home and ask an adult to help you try it out!

What do you know about Canada's Food Guide and healthy eating habits? Read on to find out what you need to stay healthy and grow.

THE GREAT CANADIAN ❖ Nutrition Challenge

Guide from Health and Welfare Canada
Quiz from *kidsworld Magazine*

Canada's Food Guide to Healthy Eating

Enjoy a variety of foods from each food group every day. Young children can choose the lower number of servings. Teenagers can choose the higher number. Most other people are in between.

| Grain Products: | Vegetables and Fruit: | Milk Products: | Meat and Alternatives: |
| 5-12 servings per day | 5-10 servings per day | 5-10 servings per day | 2-3 servings per day |

Nutrition Quiz

This is a multiple-choice quiz. After each question, there are four possible answers. Usually ONLY ONE answer is correct. But "all of the above" means the first three items may all be correct.

Directions

In your notebook, write the numbers 1 to 11. Beside each number, write the letter of the correct answer. If you get them all right, the letters spell a magic word!

1. Which meal is a good meal?
- **A** a meal with foods from all four food groups
- **B** all your favourite foods together
- **C** a meal that leaves you feeling full
- **D** a meal with food that's all one colour

2. Which drink is NOT nutritious?
- **A** milk
- **B** ginger ale
- **C** pure fruit juice
- **D** chocolate milk

3. Which meal is a good choice for breakfast?
- **O** whole grain cereal with milk
- **P** toast and peanut butter
- **Q** yogurt and fresh fruit
- **R** all of the above

4. Which snack will NOT promote cavities in your teeth?
- **A** cheese
- **B** candy
- **C** dried fruit
- **D** muffins

5. Which of these nutrients helps build bones?
- **A** protein
- **B** vitamins
- **C** calcium
- **D** fats

6. Which food is NOT a meat alternative?
- **A** lettuce
- **B** tofu
- **C** peanut butter
- **D** beans

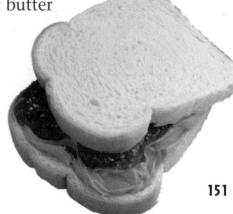

7. You need food energy to

Ⓐ stay alive

Ⓑ be good at sports

Ⓒ grow

Ⓓ all of the above

8. Which food has the most vitamin C?

Ⓐ an orange

Ⓑ an apple

Ⓒ a glass of milk

Ⓓ one serving of chicken

9. How many servings of vegetables and fruit should you have each day?

Ⓐ 1 to 2

Ⓑ 5 to10

Ⓒ 20 to 30

Ⓓ none

10. Which is most important to your health?

Ⓞ healthy eating

Ⓟ regular exercise

Ⓠ regular bedtimes

Ⓡ all of the above

11. Which vegetable can be red, green, or yellow?

Ⓐ peppers

Ⓑ carrots

Ⓒ spinach

Ⓓ eggplant

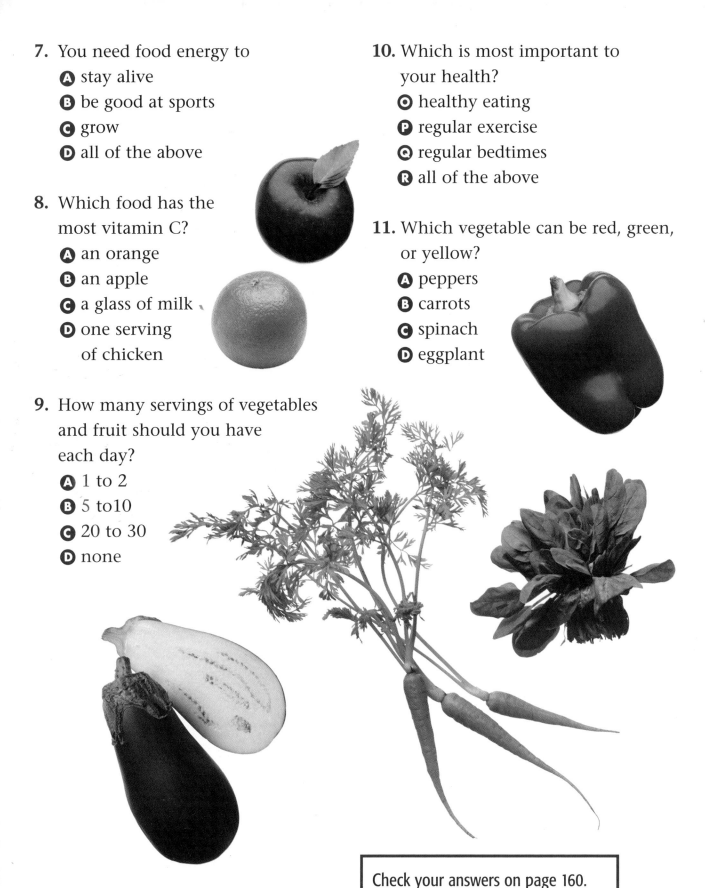

Check your answers on page 160.

FOLLOW UP

In a small group, share your answers to the quiz. In your notebook, write down any new facts you've learned.

Understanding the Selection

Healthy Eating

Copy the four food group headings into your notebook.

1. Grain Products
2. Vegetables and Fruit
3. Milk Products
4. Meat and Alternatives

Place the foods from the box under the correct heading. Look for one food that fits under all four headings. Look for one food that doesn't fit under any heading!

pepperoni pizza

sugar   **salmon**

peanut butter **bagels**

eggplant   **tofu**

potato chips   **ice cream**

Create a Quiz

Make up your own quiz. Choose one of these topics, or make up your own:

Festivals   Sports   Music

1. Write five questions about your topic.

2. Below each question, write the correct answer.

3. Add three wrong answers.

4. Mix up the answers and label them (a), (b), (c), and (d).

5. Rewrite your quiz neatly.

Try out your quiz on your friends. Did they find it easy or hard? Should you make any changes to improve your quiz?

BEFORE READING

Have you ever heard an expression and wondered where it came from? Here are the facts behind some funny food phrases.

Phrase Origins by
Marvin Terban

That Takes the Cake
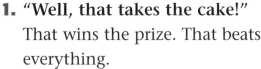

1. **"Well, that takes the cake!"**
That wins the prize. That beats everything.

- A cake was often the grand prize in a contest. In the "cake walk" contest, couples walked around a cake with high prancing steps. Judges decided which couple walked with the most graceful or original steps. The winners got to keep the cake!

2. **"He's not worth his salt."**
He's a poor worker and has not earned his salary.

- Soldiers in Ancient Rome used part of their pay to buy salt. Salt was hard to get then, but it made food taste better. If an officer thought a soldier was lazy, he said the man wasn't "worth his salt." By the way, the word **salary** comes from the Latin word for **salt**.

3. **"She's calling it sour grapes now."**
She wanted something but couldn't get it. Now she says she wouldn't have liked it even if she had gotten it.

- Aesop tells a fable about a fox on a hot day. She longed to munch on a bunch of yummy-looking grapes hanging from a vine. She jumped and leaped, but couldn't reach them. To make herself feel better, she said that the grapes were probably sour anyway.

FOLLOW UP

Which funny food phrase is your favourite? Had you heard any of these phrases before?

Matching Game

Here are six more funny food phrases. Below is a list of meanings. Which meaning matches each funny food phrase?

In your notebook, write the numbers 1 to 6. Beside each number, write the matching letter.

More Funny Food Phrases

1. "Don't bite off more than you can chew."

2. "He spilled the beans."

3. "My sister tries to butter me up."

4. "They're going bananas!"

5. "She's the apple of his eye."

6. "That's the way the cookie crumbles."

Meanings

(a) They're acting silly.

(b) That's the way life is.

(c) Don't try to do more than you are able.

(d) He let the secret out.

(e) He loves her a lot.

(f) She acts nicely when she wants something from me.

BEFORE READING

You're about to meet two circus performers. They do their act in a very special Canadian circus. Read on to discover what it is.

Human Pretzels

Profile adapted from "Science Rocks the Circus"
by **Drew McKibben** and **Diane Bailey**

Spin out, spring up, twist your body, tumble down, flip up, up, and away! That's what the daring circus artists do, and the crowd goes wild!

Everyone loves the circus, and Canada has a very special one. It's the Cirque du Soleil (Circus of the Sun) from Montréal, Québec. Unlike other circuses, Cirque du Soleil has no animals, but it does have all the colour and excitement you could want. Clowns, jugglers, tightrope walkers, acrobats, unicyclists, human towers, and bungee jumpers swirl around the tent. Costumes dazzle the eye, and music carries you to fantasy land!

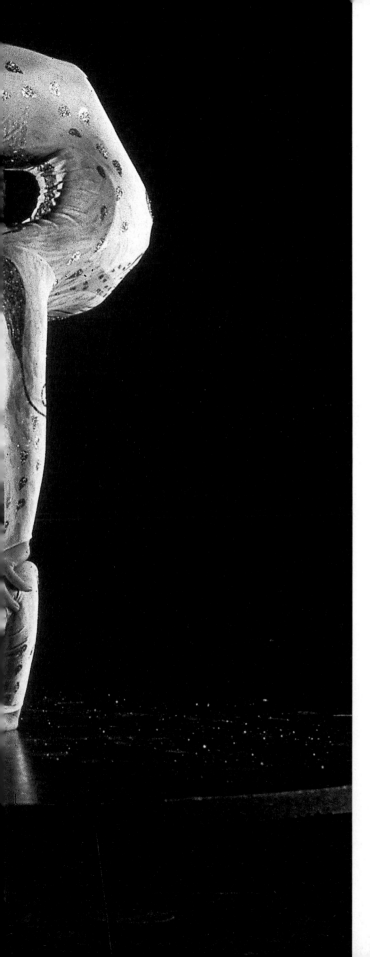

Meet two of the performers in Cirque du Soleil. They are the "human pretzels," Ulziibayar Chimed and Nomin Tseveendorj, both aged twelve. The two girls claim it doesn't hurt at all to bend and twist into these incredible shapes.

Ulzii and Nomin began learning body twists when they were five and seven years old. Later, they met and trained together at a circus school in their home country, Mongolia. For many of the moves they perform, they really have to trust each other. Was this trust hard to learn? "No," says Ulzii, "because we're friends!"

Twisting into a human pretzel is impossible for most of us. But Ulzii and Nomin are super flexible. Like all circus **contortionists***, their joints stretch and bend like elastic. It's partly training, and partly something they were born with. So please, don't try these tricks at home!

---

*contortionists: people who can twist their bodies into unnatural positions

FOLLOW UP

Would you like to do what Ulzii and Nomin do? If so, practise your gymnastic tricks. The circus may be the place for you!

Understanding the Article

Girls in a Twist

- How is Cirque du Soleil different from other circuses?
- Where did Ulzii and Nomin meet and train?
- Why do you think it's so important for them to trust each other?

Viewing the Photographs

It's easy to show what Ulzii and Nomin can do with photos. It's harder with words!

Work with a partner. Choose one of the photos. Try to describe to each other what the girls are doing.

Write a Profile

Do you know someone with a special talent? Talk to this person about his or her talent. Then write a profile of the person.

1. Make an Outline

Think of some questions like these for your interview:

- What is the person's special talent?
- How did the person learn to do this?
- How does the person share his or her talent with others?

Make notes while you're talking to the person. These notes can be your outline.

2. Write a First Draft

Following your outline, write two or three short paragraphs. You can change this version later.

3. Peer Review

Ask a partner to respond to your writing. Is the special talent well described? Does it sound interesting? What changes would improve your profile?

4. Revise Your Writing

Read your first draft aloud to yourself. Would you like to make changes?

Rewrite your profile, including your partner's suggestions.

5. Proofread Your Profile

You and your partner should now take time to correct any mistakes in your profile.

6. Publish and Share

Type your profile into a computer or print it neatly. Be sure to give it a title! Add photographs, if you have any. Read your story to friends or family.

INDEX OF AUTHORS

INDEX OF GENRES

INDEX OF ACTIVITIES

ANSWERS:

Nutrition Quiz on pages 151 and 152

1. A; 2. B; 3. R; 4. A; 5. C; 6. A; 7. D; 8. A; 9. B; 10. R; 11. A

The magic word is ABRACADABRA.